THOMAS A. DOOLEY, M.D.

DELIVER US FROM EVIL

The Story of Viet Nam's Flight to Freedom

NEW YORK

FARRAR, STRAUS AND CUDAHY

TO THE MEN OF THE U. S. NAVY AND TO THE COURAGEOUS
ESCAPEES OF NORTH VIET NAM WHO, TOGETHER, HAVE
SHOWN ME THE TRUE NOBILITY OF LIFE.

FOREWORD

by ADMIRAL ARLEIGH BURKE,

U.S. Navy, Chief of Naval Operations

The United States Navy has always been proud of its men, proud of their character, of their American ideals and convictions.

The heart of the Navy is found in its men—skilled, imaginative, courageous, alert, enthusiastic and kindly men. No organization in the world depends so much upon the individual initiative of its men as do we in the Navy.

The Navy is essentially a combat organization but one whose primary purpose is to support our government to the utmost both in peace and war. As a result, Navy men must continuously train thousands of other men to accomplish skillfully a myriad of undertakings. The Navy's training program is a never-ending chain. It teaches the real meaning of service to one's fellow men. It also teaches men to become technically proficient and to utilize the most modern tools in existence.

Today's naval traditions have been built by generations of men like young Doctor Dooley who have, served their country well under arduous and challenging circumstances. The American sailor is ofttimes (as was Doctor Dooley) confronted with situations in which proper courses of action could not have been pre-planned or pre-determined.

Therefore in his training, whether as line officer, doctor or boatswain's mate, each individual must have prepared himself to assume responsibility and to act in accordance with his best judgment. Every Navy man must know that the life of his ship, and the success of his country, may sometimes depend upon his willingness and his ability to act boldly and independently for the common good.

Hence sailors will read with pride, as will all Americans, the courageous exploits of the young lieutenant, Doctor Dooley. His humanitarian actions are the kind of good deeds that will remain indelibly impressed in people's hearts—good deeds that neither propaganda nor brain-washing will ever stain.

Through the tireless work of his small naval unit in the huge refugee camps of the hostile and turbulent North Viet Nam country, he has won for America the love and admiration of thousands and thousands of refugees who passed through these camps on their historic march to freedom.

Lieutenant Dooley, a naval medical officer on independent duty, contributed greatly to the welfare of mankind and to an understanding of the fundamental principles of the United States, as he participated in this epoch-making period of world history. In DELIVER US FROM EVIL he has written that story with freshness, clarity and force. It is a story that will be told and re-told.

It is a story of which the United States Navy is proud.

CONTENTS

DELIVER US FROM EVIL

CHAPTER I

ENSIGN POTTS CHANGES
HIS MIND

The Hickham Field airport terminal was jammed with military personnel and their dependents. November in Hawaii is lovely; when a light misty rain is falling, the Islands are enchanting. And I was going home. I was going *home*. Two weeks in Hawaii, winding up my two-year overseas stint, went fast and gave me two great moments. The second moment occurred right at Hickham Field.

The scene of my first was a U. S. Navy holy-of-holies— the Command Conference Room for Pacific Fleet Headquarters at Pearl Harbor. There I was to brief Admiral Felix B. Stump's staff on my recent experiences in Southeast Asia. Admiral Stump was the Commander-in-Chief of the Military Forces of the Pacific. I was just a twenty-eight-year old Lieutenant (recently junior grade) in the Navy Medical Corps, in command of nothing whatsoever.

But I had had rich duty in the Orient. I had been stationed in the city of Haiphong, in North Viet Nam, Indo-

3

China, and assisted in the epic "Passage to Freedom" that moved some 600,000 Vietnamese from the Communist North to the non-Communist South.

Indo-China had been a French colony. But on May 7, 1954, after eight years of bloody colonial and civil war, the key fortress of Dien Bien Phu had fallen to the Communists, and soon thereafter, at Geneva, the Red victory was nailed down in a peace treaty that arbitrarily split an ancient country in half. One of the treaty's terms said that, if they wished, non-Communists in the north would be allowed to migrate to the south. Hundreds of thousands desperately wished to do so and most of those who made the trip traveled through Haiphong. And that was where I came in.

Needless to say, Admiral Stump's staff had received regular reports on the operations at Haiphong, probably with frequent enough mentions of a young Irish-American doctor named Dooley. But evidently they wanted more, or at any rate Admiral Stump thought they did. So I was ordered to stop over on the way home to deliver a briefing, which is a lecture in uniform.

It was delivered in a room that collects stars. On this day, when I addressed some eighty officers for one packed hour, I counted sixteen of those stars on the collars in the front row. Captains filled the next few rows. Commanders brought up the rear.

Rank doesn't scare me too much, but when it gangs up on a man in this wholesale fashion it does shake him a little. But I told these men about the hordes of refugees from

4

terror-ridden North Viet Nam and how we "processed" them for evacuation. I told them how these pathetic crowds of men, women and children escaped from behind the Bamboo Curtain, which was just on the other side of Haiphong, and of those who tried to escape and failed. I told of the medical aid given them in great camps at Haiphong and of how, in due course, they were packed into small craft for a four-hour trip down the Red River, to be reloaded onto American ships for a journey of two days and three nights 1000 miles down the coast to the city of Saigon, in South Viet Nam.

I told them individual tales of horror that I had heard so many nights in candlelit tents, in the monsoon rains of that South China Sea area. I even got in some complaints. Why hadn't certain missions been carried out more effectively? Why had American naval policy dictated such and such a course? So for one hour I talked. They all listened intently.

I suppose one measure of a lecturer's hold on his audience is the length of time it takes for the questions that follow his speech. I must have had a pretty good hold because the questioning lasted more than seventy minutes. Finally three stars in the front row spoke up. "All right, Dr. Dooley," he said. "You have given us a vivid picture and told us moving stories of courage and nobility. You have also raised a lot of objections. But you have not offered one solution or one suggestion on what we can or should do in the still-free parts of Southeast Asia."

I responded, perhaps a bit unfairly, that two small

5

stripes could hardly presume to offer solutions, if indeed ther are any, to three big stars. My job was to take care of backaches and boils.

Then came my first big moment in Hawaii—the Walter Mitty dream moment that every junior officer has dreamed of since the Navy began. How often I had sat at table in the ship's wardroom saying, "Well, if I were running this outfit. . . ." Or "Why the devil didn't the Admiral do it this way?" And now the Admiral was saying, "Well, Dooley, what would *you* do if *you* were wearing the stars?"

I took the plunge with a few suggestions, low level and not necessarily new.

"Sir," I said, "I think that American officers ashore in Asia should always wear their uniforms. I think that American Aid goods should always be clearly marked. I think we should define democracy in Asia so that it will be clearer and more attractive than the definitions Asians get from the Communists."

I said a lot more which, to be perfectly truthful, I can no longer remember, and even as I held forth I was worried about my cockiness. You get neither applause nor boos from such an audience, merely a curt "Thank you, Doctor." The only punishment meted out to me when the show was over was a request to repeat the briefing to a lot of other audiences in Hawaii, military and civilian.

Only one man besides myself attended all my briefings. He was the hapless Ensign Potts, a spit-and-polish young officer five months out of Annapolis. He had been assigned

6

to help me with the myriad little things I had to do on my lecture tour of Hawaii.

Ensign Potts baffled me. He saluted me every time I turned around. Riding in a Navy car with me he would invariably sit in the front seat with the driver. When I would ask him to sit in the back with me his response would be: "No thank you, sir, I think it will be better if I sit up front." Sometimes, after I had delivered a lecture in the evening, I would ask Potts to come to the beach with me for a swim. "No, sir, thank you," he would say. "I had better go back to Officers' Quarters."

As we drove to Hickham Air Force base for my flight home, I again asked Potts to sit in the rear seat with me. "No thank you, sir," he started to say, but by this time Ensign Potts was getting on my nerves.

"Mr. Potts," I said, "get in this back seat. I want to talk to you. That is an order."

Stiffly and reluctantly, he obeyed.

"Potts," I said, "what the hell's wrong with you—or with me? I think I get along with most people fairly well, but obviously you don't like me. What's up?"

"May I speak frankly, sir?" he asked.

"Hell yes," I said.

"Then, sir," he said, "allow me to say that I am fed up with you. I am fed up with your spouting off about a milling mass of humanity, about the orphans of a nation, a great sea of souls and all the rest of that junk. And what I am most fed up with, and damn mad about, is that most of the people you spout at seem to believe you."

7

Ensign Potts stopped a moment to observe my reaction. When he saw I was listening, he continued:

"You talk of love, about how we must not fight Communist lust with hate, must not oppose tyrannical violence with more violence, nor Communist destruction with atomic war. You preach of love, understanding and helpfulness.

"That's not the Navy's job. We've got military responsibilities in this cockeyed world. We've got to perform our duties sternly and without sentiment. That's what we've been trained for.

"I don't believe your prescription will work. I believe that the only answer is preventive war."

Evidently he had thought a lot about it. He explained that some 200 targets in Red Russia, Red China and the satellite nations could be bombed simultaneously and that this would destroy the potential of Communism's production for war. Then a few more weeks of all-out war would destroy Communist forces already in existence.

Sure, the toll of American lives would be heavy, but the sacrifice would be justified to rid mankind of the Communist peril before it grew strong enough to lick us. For that matter, maybe it was too late already.

Slowly Dooley was beginning to understand Potts. The Ensign had nothing against me personally; he just didn't like what I was preaching. He himself had a radically different set of ideas, and many Americans, I suppose, share his views. I do not.

The Ensign had not yet said his full say. "Dr. Dooley," he concluded, "the oldest picture known to modern man,

8

one of the oldest pieces of art in the world, is on the walls
of a cave in France. It shows men with bows and arrows
engaged in man's customary pastime of killing his fellow
man. And this will go on forever. Prayers are for old
women. They have no power."

With this he fell silent, sucked in a deep breath and
slumped in his seat. He had vented his hostility and was
appeased.

Just then I noticed that our car was not moving. We had
arrived at the terminal, but the sailor chauffering the car
was too engrossed in our conversation to interrupt. Potts
and I stepped out, disagreeing but friends at last.

And that brings me to the second of my two big moments
in Hawaii.

I stood in the misty perfumed rain at the terminal. I was
heading home. Things would be quiet now. They would be
pleasant and uneventful. I was going to sleep, eat, and then
eat and sleep again. There would be no turmoil. No hatred.
No sorrow. No atrocities. No straining with foreign languages (I can speak Vietnamese and French, but they take
a toll on the nervous system).

The terminal building at Hickham is immense. Pre-
occupied with thoughts of going home, I did not hear the
first shout, but the second one came through loud and
clearly. From the other end of the waiting-room someone
was yelling: *"Chao Ong Bac Sy My,"* which in Vietnamese
means, "Hi, American doctor."

I turned around and was enmeshed in a pair of strong
young arms that pinioned my own arms to my side. A

9

Vietnamese Air Force cadet was hugging me tight and blubbering all over my coat. He was a short, handsome lad of perhaps sixteen. Squeezing the breath out of my chest, he was talking so fast that it was difficult to understand what he said. Suddenly there were about two dozen other olive-skinned youngsters in cadet uniforms swarming around me, shaking my hands and pounding me on the back as an air-hammer pounds a pavement. They were all wearing the uniform of the Vietnamese Air Force. And everyone concerned was bawling all over the place.

"Don't you remember me, American Doctor? Don't you remember?" asked the boy who still had me pinioned in his bear-hug.

"Of course I do," I lied—who could remember one face among those hundreds of thousands?—but behold! the lie turned into truth and the old familiar gloom came over me. The boy had no left ear. Where it should have been, there was only an ugly scar. I had made that scar. I had amputated that ear. I might not remember this particular boy, but I would never forget the many boys and girls of whom he had been one. The ear amputation was their hideous trademark.

"You're from Bao Lac," I said, disentangling myself from his embrace. Pointing to others in the group, I added, "And so are you, and you and you."

Each of them also had a big scar where an ear should have been. I remembered that in the Roman Catholic province of Bao Lac, near the frontier of China, the Com-

10

munist Viet Minh often would tear an ear partially off with a pincer like a pair of pliers and leave the ear dangling. That was one of penalties for the crime of listening to evil words. The evil words were the words of the Lord's Prayer: "Our Father, Who art in Heaven, hallowed be Thy name . . . . Give us this day our daily bread . . . . and deliver us from evil. . . ." How downright treasonable, to ask God for bread instead of applying to the proper Communist authorities! How criminal to imply that the new People's Republic was an evil from which one needed deliverance! A mutilated ear would remind such scoundrels of the necessity for re-education.

The boy spoke of his escape from North Viet Nam in November of 1954, when he had come to my camp. There I had amputated the stump of his ear, dissected the skin surfaces of the external canal, then pulled the skin of the scalp and that of the face together and sutured them. The tension was great on the suture line, and I knew the scar would be wide and ugly. But, with the limited time and equipment available, I had no alternative. Would he hear again from that ear? Never. Only from the other ear would he ever hear words, evil or holy.

All of the Vietnamese youngsters now in the Hawaiian terminal had passed through our camps at Haiphong, and many of them bore this trademark. I had put them on small French craft or on sampans which carried them to American ships to be taken to Saigon. There those who had reached the age of sixteen were old enough to join the

11

newly created Air Force of Viet Nam. At sixteen they were men, preparing to regain the north half of their country from the Communists.

Under an American Military Aid Program, this contingent was going to Texas to be trained as mechanics. At the airport in Hawaii they had spotted the American doctor who had helped them a year earlier. They remembered him. I remembered only the scars.

A fairly large crowd, mostly Americans, had been attracted by our noisy and tearful reunion. Some people wanted to know what it was all about. This seemed as good a time as any to begin "briefing" my fellow-citizens, and I made a speech. I told them about these youngsters and their valor; I told them where I had come from and what I had seen, and then I satisfied their curiosity as to why most of these air cadets had only one ear apiece. I suspect I did not succeed in keeping the tears out of my voice. Soon many of those who had been staring at us and who now understood began to find their vision clouding up, just as mine was clouded. Not in many a year had that number of tears hit the deck at Hickham.

And among those who wept and did not bother to hide it was Ensign Potts. The same young officer who half an hour before had scoffed at my softness.

"Mr. Potts!" I commanded. "Pull yourself together, sir."

He came over, grinning through the tears, and shook my hand.

"Mr. Potts," I said, "don't you think these kids would

12

do anything, even at the risk of their lives, because of the way they feel about one American?"

In all the honesty of his enthusiastic heart, Ensign Potts replied: "Yes, Doctor, I think they would. Perhaps you are right. Perhaps there *is* a special power in love."

CHAPTER II

THIRTY-SIX BRANDS OF SOAP

The Vietnamese cadets had been caught in the inevitable foul-up. They had been at Hickham for days with no one to look after them. Since they knew no English, they had just been wandering around the terminal to kill time. I tracked down the Air Force officer in charge; he told me the kids were due to leave on a flight that night. I asked if I could be put aboard the same plane. That, it seemed, was impossible. Suddenly my new friend, Ensign Potts, moved into line with all guns blazing.

"Sir," he roared, inaccurately, "Doctor Dooley is Admiral Stump's guest, and I have authority to speak for the Admiral. The doctor can have the Admiral's own plane if he wants it. It seems to me the least the Air Force can do is to put him on that lousy flight."

So the Air Force put me on the flight, which wasn't so lousy at that.

The big Constellation was filled with soldiers, sailors and marines. When we were airborne I told them a little about their fellow passengers, the twenty-six olive-garbed Vietnamese. I called up my cadets one by one and asked each to tell his story while I translated. My captive audience, at first indifferent, was soon entranced.

Then I asked the Vietnamese to sing some of their mountain songs. The Tonkin mountain music is melodious, almost eerie, something like the ancient Hebrew liturgical chants. The cadets sang and the Americans on the plane listened with attention.

Next I asked the U. S. servicemen to sing some American songs. "OK, Doc," a sailor said, "how about *Shake, Rattle and Roll?*" The title was tough to translate into Vietnamese, but the singing was great. And so was the singing of *Home on the Range, There's Nothing Like a Dame* and *Deep in the Heart of Texas.*

Thus passed the flight, with a great good deal of singing and laughter. When we finally came in over the Golden Gate, the Americans shifted seats to let the "foreigners" sit by the windows and excitedly tried to explain the sights below by gestures and sign language. I felt good inside.

We landed at Travis Air Force Base near San Francisco. There I watched my fellow passengers file off the plane, each soldier, sailor and marine with a cadet in tow. After we were processed, the Vietnamese had ten hours to kill before taking off for Texas. The Air Force provided a bus and some of the U. S. servicemen volunteered to come along while I took the kids sightseeing .

When I returned to San Francisco it was as though I had been away for ages. We take too many things for

15

granted in our American way of life; when we are absent from them for a year or two, they become engrossing, wonderful, slightly incredible. Why, hey, say! I learned that American ingenuity had developed an automobile with gears that can be shifted by pushing a button, and a television set on which programs can be turned off and on by sighting it with a Buck Rogers type of ray gun. Such wonders almost floored me because now I saw them through the eyes of the kids.

Downtown San Francisco made them bug-eyed with wonder. When we went into an all-night drugstore for milk-shakes, the Vietnamese wandered around as if in fairyland. Under the glaring lights, at their insistence, I described the contents of some of those colorful packages which were stacked on the shelves. One section was devoted to soaps; a cadet counted thirty-six different brands. "Please explain the differences between them," he said to me, and that one had me stumped. The first bar of soap he had ever seen was one I had given him in Haiphong—and I had only one kind. All his life, until then, he had used a fat preparation. To him, that was soap. An American sailor came to my rescue. "Tell him they have thirty-six different smells," he said, and I translated to the cadet's satisfaction.

We finally returned to Travis Airport where I loaded my charges on a plane bound for the deep heart of Texas. We said "So long" and they thanked me again, individually and collectively. But I think I owed them some thanks too. For one thing, they had taught me to appreciate afresh some of the assets of my country. And not just the material assets either.

At Haiphong, to get supplies for the miserable refugees, I had done some shameless begging, seeking this, that or the other thing from American groups, business concerns and individuals. Now I wanted to spend part of my leave in thanking the people who had responded to this Operation Hat-in-Hand—the pharmaceutical companies, surgical supply houses and such outfits as the International Rescue Committee and the Youth of All Nations.

While I was on the West Coast, I decided to visit the San Diego high school whose senior class had sent my refugees bundles of clothes and other necessities. The principal and teachers arranged it so that I addressed the assembled classes of several San Diego schools.

I looked out over that sea of fresh young faces and felt older than Father Abraham. They were noisy kids, some of them dressed in faded blue jeans and leather jackets, some of the girls wearing full-blown sweaters, and many of the boys with those long duck-butt haircuts. When I stepped out on the platform, wearing my uniform and ribbons, there was a bedlam of wolf-calls and whistles and stomping feet.

They were tough, so I decided to shoot the works. I gave them the whole sordid story of the refugee camps, the Communist atrocities, the "Passage to Freedom," and the perilous future of southern Viet Nam. I talked for an hour —you can see I was getting to be quite a windbag—and you could have heard a pin drop.

17

When I was through, they asked questions for another hour—earnest, intelligent questions that kept me on my toes. Toward the close, there was one little girl in the rear who had to come down front in order to be heard. She couldn't have been more than thirteen and she took a wad of gum from her mouth before asking her question with intense seriousness.

"Doctor Dooley, what can we boys and girls of the Lincoln Memorial High School *really do* to help improve the social, economic and political situation in Southeast Asia?"

Now that *is* a stopper! But dear little girl, put back your gum and don't be ashamed. I haven't met a single American who hasn't asked something like that once he has heard the facts.

I have no magic formula to offer. What do *I* know about foreign aid in billion-dollar packages? But I do know that American aid, used wisely and generously by individuals, on a people-to-people basis, can create bonds of friendship that will be hard to sever. And we have several million willing American hands around the world, if we want to use them—not in the Navy alone, but in all the services overseas. We can still serve the folks back home—if they want us to—as instruments of the sympathy, generosity and understanding that are hallmarks of the American character.

Unless these intangibles are conveyed to Asian people plainly, I'm afraid the costly programs of material aid are often wasted. And they needn't be. My meager resources and lame efforts in Indo-China did not win the people's hearts, although I know they helped. What turned the trick, when the trick was turned, were those words: *"Day La Vien Tro My"* ("This is American Aid")—and all that those words conveyed. Let us stop being afraid to speak of compassion, and generosity. Christ said it all in the three words of His great commandment: "Love one another."

I then took a train to St. Louis, my home town, because I wanted to see America's fields and mountains, her canyons and plains. I even sat up most of the night looking out the window. I was home. I was back in America—though truly I had never left her at all. She was in my heart. I wore her insignia on my hat, her bold eagle and shield over her Navy's anchors.

At home in St. Louis I answered a thousand questions. How did that evacuation of the north get started? What are these people really like? How the hell did a young man like *you* get into it? What did the President of Viet Nam mean when he said, "Doctor Dooley, you are the only American I have ever met who could speak my language. . . . You are beloved by my people. You were the first American most of them ever saw and by knowing and loving you they grew to understand the American people." If as he said they loved you so damned much, why did they beat you up?

The answers are long and involved. They can only be found by reviewing the whole story of the evacuation, from day one to the end of the eleventh month.

19

CHAPTER III

NEW CARGO FOR THE
U.S.S. MONTAGUE

One night, in the spring of 1955, I lay sleepless and sweltering in the dying city of Haiphong, north Viet Nam, asking myself the question that has taunted so many young Americans caught in far-away places "Whatinhell am *I* doing here?"

None of the answers that came to mind seemed wholly satisfying. I was on this weird mission under the Bamboo Curtain because—in a way—I had asked for it. Each month the Navy offered me the chance to quit and go back aboard a nice clean ship and perhaps go home. Yet each month I volunteered to stay on in this nightmare for still another thirty days. Why? In my depressed mood I cursed myself for a damned fool.

For as long as I could remember, I had wanted to be a doctor. Now, at twenty-eight, I was an M.D., although a very green one. Moreover, I was a Navy doctor, an added distinction I had coveted since I served as a hospital corpsman in the United States Navy in 1944-46. Finally, I was one young doctor who did *not* lack patients. God knows, I had more cases on my unskilled hands at the moment than the most seasoned doctor has any right to handle.

Out there, in the 140-odd tents of the quagmire I called Camp de la Pagode (there wasn't a pagoda within miles) were more than 12,000 wretched, sick and often horribly maimed Vietnamese, most of them either very young or very old, who were fleeing from the Communists of northern Viet Nam, hoping to reach the doubtful security of Saigon. Many thousands had previously passed through my camps and the number would run into the hundreds of thousands before the tragedy ended.

Sure, I had long known about the fall of Dien Bien Phu, in which world Communism had scored another resounding triumph. At the Yokosuka Naval Hospital in Japan, where I had been stationed only a couple of months, I had followed this news in a casual, impersonal way, like everyone else. If I was a little more interested than most were, it was only because Indo-China was a French colony; I had studied in Paris at the Sorbonne and had an interest in everything French.

Yet, because of Dien Bien Phu, here I was, more by accident than by merit, in practical command of the medical aspects of the gigantic job of evacuation at Haiphong, and its periphery in the Tonkin Delta.

For me, tropical medicine had been a drowsy course at St. Louis University Medical School. Yet now I was crowding more practice in malaria, yaws, beri-beri, smallpox, leprosy and cholera into a month than most doctors see in a long lifetime.

I was only a fledgling surgeon, but already I had performed operations which the textbooks never mention.

21

What do you do for children who have had chopsticks driven into their inner ears? Or for old women whose brittle collar-bones have been shattered by rifle butts? How do you treat an old priest who has had nails driven into his skull to make a travesty of the Crown of Thorns?

I had never before borne real responsibility or authority. But now I had to provide shelter and food, sanitation and some human solace to a flood of humanity, undernourished, exhausted, bewildered and pitifully frightened. My primary task was medical—to stamp out contagious diseases before these hordes boarded our transport vessels, and so to protect our crews against epidemics. But there was no ducking the huge problems of housekeeping and administration for the shifting camp population, normally between 10,000 and 15,000 persons.

And, maybe because I am a glutton for punishment, I chose not to duck larger tasks not set down in my instructions. One was to help refugees to reach our evacuation zone. They had been told, formally, in the Geneva compact, that they could be evacuated when, as and if they wished. But it turned out that they had been told a lie. Another of my tasks was to teach at least some of the refugees, in the brief time they were in my charge, to understand and trust Americans.

I had to do these things, moreover, across barriers of suspicion, fear and often hatred of Americans cunningly instilled by Communist propaganda. My assignment brought me face to face with misery on a horrifying scale, with hideous atrocities—but also with quiet courage, simple nobility and, above all, the miracle of a faith in God that takes the risks of torture and death in its stride.

Yes, cocky young Dooley, whom the profs at medical school had ticketed as a future "society doctor," was learning things the hard way, but he was learning at last. At Notre Dame they had tried hard to teach me philosophy. Now out here in this hell-hole I had learned many profound and practical facts about the true nature of man. I understood the inherent quality that enables tough, loud-mouthed sailors to become tender nurses for sick babies and dying old men. I had seen inhuman torture and suffering elevate weak men to great heights of spiritual nobility. I know now why organized godlessness never can kill the divine spark which burns within even the humblest human.

That night, in my tent at Haiphong, I tossed fitfully on a sweaty cot until, just before dawn, I heard Boatswain's Mate Norman Baker—"lately from New Hampshire, sir, and proud of it"—stumble into my tent.

"Better get moving, Doc," he said. "We've got another batch—800 or maybe a thousand more."

From Baker's tone, I could tell that the newcomers would be like all the rest—filthy, starving, diseased, and maimed in God knows what manner.

Groping for a flashlight and pushing my swollen feet into a pair of muddy boondockers, I instinctively began murmuring the *Our Father*, as I had every day since childhood: "And deliver us from evil." I had to pause in the darkness. Yes, O God, that is the people's prayer—to be

23

delivered from evil. At that moment I think I sensed, however dimly, the purpose behind my being in Indo-China.

The evacuation of north Viet Nam really began, at least for me, in the Philippines.

In the first week of August, 1954, with the one-and-a-half stripes of a Lieutenant (j.g.) on my sleeve, I was assigned to the *U. S. S. Montague*, AKA (Auxiliary Cargo Attack) 98, for thirty days of what the Navy calls TAD. Those letters mean Temporary Additional Duty, and they also happen to be the initials of my name: Thomas A. Dooley. We were to take part in amphibious exercises, and practice landings on the Philippine beaches. Soon we had conquered all the undefended beaches in the area.

(The duty seemed so temporary that I allowed a Navy nurse in Yokosuka, Japan, my last station, to drive my new convertible while I was gone and I told my roommate that he could wear my brand-new civilian suit. When I got back to Japan, eleven months later, there were 20,000 additional miles on the speedometer and as for the new suit—well, I couldn't have worn it anyway. I had lost sixty of my 180 pounds.)

For a Navy doctor, the maneuvers were not too strenuous and there was amusement on shore. I planned to devote my life to the U. S. Navy and this was my first big chance to get better acquainted with ships and sailors and the sea that is their stern mistress. I had seen plenty of ships before —the *Queen Elizabeth*, the *Queen Mary*, the *Independence*. But in my mind they couldn't compare with an AKA. I admit the *Montague* was not as luxurious as the *Queen Elizabeth* and certainly it did not have the cocktail space of the *Independence*. But to me it was important—important because it was my first ship and important because of the friendships I made. In the Navy friendships are easily made—and difficult to forget.

After we had scrambled down landing nets and stormed ashore repeatedly for a couple of weeks, we reloaded equipment and put in at the big naval base on Subic Bay, across the island from Manila. There most of us were doing "club time" exercises—swimming, sunning, sleeping, or drinking gin and tonic—when our breathing spell in the breathless Philippine summer heat was cut short, very short.

Task Force 90 was ordered to "proceed on 12 August 1954 to Haiphong, Viet Nam, Indo-China, anchor in stream and await instructions." Operation "Passage to Freedom" was getting under steam, we were part of it, and we were not to discuss it with anyone. That last command was easy to obey. Few of us knew anything about Indo-China other than the fact that it was south of China and east of India. And we knew even less of this "Passage of Freedom." Who or what was passing to freedom, and where, and why?

Our "Op Order," the Operation Order detailing a mission, was not to reach us until the day we dropped anchor off Haiphong. The Admiral in charge of the Task Force that included the *Montague* knew the answers, but he did not know them soon enough to draft the order before we left the Philippines.

25

What we did know, however, was that we were to prepare our ship to transport 2,000 people. We were ordered to prepare for this new type of cargo in two days, then sail. The trip would take another two days. Total, four days. Four days in which to transform the *Montague*, a cargo ship built to transport tanks and trucks, into a ship to carry a cargo of humans, 2,000 at a time.

As the ship's medical officer, I should have sensed the significance of the worried look on Captain William Cox's face; but I was a neophyte, full of animal spirits, and this grueling, around-the-clock chore sounded like a lark.

What we did during the two days at Subic Bay and the two days under sail was unbelievable. We converted this ship into a passenger liner, though without many of the ocean-going luxury items, to be sure.

An AKA is about 460 feet long and has five large holds, with three levels to each hold. These are used to store the trucks, tanks and other vehicles for amphibious landings. There is no ventilation in the holds and the only openings are the hatches or covers which must be replaced after the cargo is loaded. On the tops of the hatches the ship carries landing craft.

Normally, after the lowest level of each hold is loaded, its hatch is closed and the level above gets its cargo. For the Passage to Freedom these holds had to be converted to accomodate men, women and children—something the designers had never anticipated. It was hardly an ideal arrangement.

The first thing we did was to remove the ladders from

deck levels and place them between the levels of the holds to provide entry into and egress from their deep recesses. Wooden staircases were constructed for the holds when all the metal ones were used up. Water hoses were rigged into all the holds, along with fans and such other accessories as we could muster. The hatches, of course, could not be left open, for fear that people would plunge down three levels; but every other hatch board was removed to allow air to filter down.

Each division officer tried to imagine what he would need in the way of supplies, and then we headed for the supply depot at Subic Bay. Whatever we thought we needed we piled aboard, overlooking formalities and showing a fine disregard for Supply Corps rules and regulations. Aboard went tons of rice, hundreds of crates of sardines, thousands of drinking cups, 60-gallon drums, empty paint cans to serve as portable toilets, tons of sawdust to be strategically deployed in boxes for the seasick.

We sailed out of Subic Bay on the designated date, full of rice and mystery and scuttlebutt. Every sailor and every officer had the inside dope and was willing to share it with someone else in return for a pledge of secrecy.

Officers held roundtable discussions in the wardroom. Enlisted men held discussions around a stanchion on the fantail. Then we had combined conferences in which each contributed his piddling bit of information. If all this jawing did nothing else, it at least brought one thing to light quite vividly—how little most of us knew about Southeast Asia.

27

We scoured all the reference books we could find aboard the ship. We dug through old magazines. We looked everywhere for information on Indo-China. We found pitifully little.

Meanwhile, at sea, the ship resounded with hammering and sawing and the shouting of orders. All the facilities ingenuity could contrive were provided for our prospective guests. Sixty-gallon canvas "Lister" bags for drinking water were hung in the holds. Oil drums were scoured and filled with water for washing.

But Captain Cox's masterpiece was the latrine system. Oil drums were split lengthwise, welded end to end, and topped by wooden seats in which the carpenters cut holes of various sizes. When the job was finished, the skipper made an inspection.

I'll never know whether his primary concern was for Vietnamese buttocks, or the tremendous job of splinter-picking that seemed about to devolve on the ship's doctor. But he ordered blocks of sandpaper and stood by until the men had rubbed those latrine seats satin smooth. As things turned out, however, he might have spared the sailors their trouble. Asian toilet habits are decidedly different, as we were to learn.

Now our reconversion was complete. Now we were ready. But for what?

Not until much later did we realize that we were the advance guard in the largest evacuation ever undertaken by the U. S. Navy.

CHAPTER IV

THE REFUGEES COME ABOARD

The *Montague* glided into the surrealist beauty of the Baie d'Along on August 14, 1954. On the same day several other ships anchored in the stream. By August 15th there were five ships lined up in this slit among the bay's crags and rocks. We were at Position 1; the *Menard*, another cargo ship, was at Position 5.

Anxiously we waited for our first view of the refugees. What would they be like? How many of them would there be? What kind of diseases would they bring with them? We soon found out.

I tried to imagine what conditions must be with hordes of people pouring into the city of Haiphong, beyond the bay four hours up river, waiting to be carried out to these strange ships standing offshore. Little did I realize that, just beyond that shoreline, lay an ordeal which would scar my memory for a lifetime.

Then I heard a shout and saw the men pointing to a small LCT slowly ploughing along in the angry swells.

29

Such small craft are built to transport four or five tanks and a few dozen men. Their overall length is less than 150 feet. As this one pulled alongside, I looked down into the open deck with horror. I know horror is a strong word, but there were more than a thousand people huddled on the deck, close-packed like fowl in a crate, wet, seasick and exposed to a brutal sun. They were numb with fright. Among them were a multitude of babies.

When the LCT arrived at the side of our ship, huge by comparison, an open gangway was lowered to its deck. This was secured as firmly as possible, fighting the swells and sickening rolls of the bay. The refugees were told to come up. I could see them hesitate, in fear. I supposed that it was merely dread of the unknown. Later I learned that the trouble was more specific—they were in mortal fear of the savage, inhuman Americans against whom they had been very often and very effectively warned.

One old man, probably one of their esteemed elders, took the lead. He started painfully up. He wore a conical straw hat and in one hand clutched a slender brown-crusted bamboo pipe. In the other hand, even more tightly, he held a chipped frame—a picture of the Blessed Virgin. It was clear that these were his most prized possessions. In fact, they were nearly all the possessions he had.

For a few steps he came on bravely, then looked down at the swells smashing inches below the steps. One look was enough. He froze where he stood. When he looked up, many things showed in his wizened face. There was starvation, all too obvious; there was fright at the booming sea; there was sheer terror of what lay ahead.

He was hunched over as if heavily burdened. When, nervously, he removed his hat, his scalp showed patches of scaling fungus. His ribs stood out sharply, stretching the skin of his chest to shiny tautness. I had never before seen such utter dejection. Could this be Viet Nam?

A white-capped sailor went down the steps; he wanted to help, repugnant as the thought of touching that old fellow must have been. But when he did touch the man, it was as if the grandfather had felt the hand of an executioner. Only the press of the people behind finally forced him to mount the rest of the steps to our deck. His trembling fingers were barely able to hold a numbered card another sailor handed him before he was urged, gently, away from the ship's rail.

We stopped the line after a few refugees had come aboard and put a canvas cover over and under the accommodation ladder so that they would not see the ocean breaking beneath the open steps. This, we hoped, would lessen their terror. Nevertheless the others, equally miserable, entered the ladder-tunnel with apprehension.

Many of them carried long balanced poles with large shallow baskets at each end. In these they carried everything they owned. Usually they had some clothes, always a rice bowl and chopsticks, invariably a religious object—a crucifix, statue or sacred picture.

On and on they came through that cavernous tunnel, some of them with eyes lowered, as if not daring to look

31

at us. They had children on their backs and in their arms; even the older kids toted babies. The children were given a tag which, when presented later, entitled them to milk, a nearly unheard-of luxury. The little ones were sweet, and wide-eyed and grave. And very frightened. I saw a sailor, to lighten a mother's load, pick up a brown little bundle of baby and mutter, "God, this kid smells awful."

Then the last of this group of refugees was aboard and the French LCT pulled away with an obvious air of relief. A second French craft pulled alongside and the dismal exchange was repeated.

Somehow, in the confusion, our guests managed to haul aboard a huge barrel of stinking oil. I took one whiff and ordered it tossed overboard. Too late, I learned that the rancid oil was considered a delicacy, indispensable to Tonkinese cookery.

Now more than 2,000 Tonkinese were started on their passage to freedom, the first of the hundreds of thousands who would depart from this harbor before the Bamboo Curtain finally fell. They had made a wholly free choice in tearing up century-old roots and abandoning revered ancestral graves. For the right to continue to worship their God—the decisive motive in nine cases out of ten—they had given up their rice paddies, their homes, their beloved native villages. What lay ahead of them in the south, which would be almost a foreign land to Tonkin Delta folk? Indeed, would these big-nosed and strangely dressed white men ever deliver them to the south at all?

They had been told in great detail by followers of Ho

32

Chi Minh—the fabled Ho Chi Minh who was playing ball with Moscow but whom many of them still regarded as a patriotic nationalist—that Americans were scarcely human. The whole evacuation they were told, was a trap. American sailors would throw the old people overboard, cut off the right hands of the newborn, and sell the comely girls as concubines to capitalists. They had seen "pictures" —crude but vivid drawings on propaganda leaflets—of just such white-capped sailors as those on this big ship roasting a child alive, presumably for breakfast.

Small wonder that there was not a smiling face, young or old, among these thousands as they clambered awkwardly into the ship's cavernous belly with their sorry belongings. So it seemed a heart-warming miracle, hours later, to notice the blossoming of shy smiles here and there, first among the children, and then among their elders too. The mood of our guests was becoming more tranquil.

We now notified the galley that they would have the mammoth task of feeding these thousands. A number of comparatively clean and healthy-looking Vietnamese—and they were not easy to find—were selected to help serve the food. We planned to serve only twice a day, but since the second meal ran into the first, the lines were continuous. Vitamin deficiences were general, and this was a chance for the Vietnamese to eat their fill, perhaps the first in months.

We cooked the rice in our own fashion, nice and fluffy. Embarrassingly, we discovered that the refugees did not like rice cooked our way. They preferred it when it looked like an inedible ball of congealed mash. When they finally got it that way, they would take extra helpings and press it into sticky chunks to be tucked into their bundles.

Finally the last refugee was aboard and the accommodation ladder hoisted. The "Ready to get underway" reports were submitted to the Skipper, the screws churned the blue-green water and the *Montague,* with its strange cargo, embarked for the south.

Soon the heat became intense and the stench almost overpowering. There was sickness throughout the ship. There were "honey buckets" for toilets in every hold, as well as large latrine troughs on the decks, but at first the refugees did not understand how to use them properly and they just didn't. It wasn't long before Captain Cox called me to his bridge and said, mournfully, "Dooley, look at my latrines!" I looked and howled with insubordinate laughter. There, answering nature's call, were eight or ten refugees, perching on the seats with their feet rather than with the usual portion of their anatomy. That was their way, and there was nothing we could do about it.

With the help of a French-speaking priest and several elders (called mandarins), we tried to make the ship's rules known. This water was for drinking, that water for washing, and so on. As we lectured them I had to struggle to control my nausea. These people were filthy, scabrous, often covered with open sores. They bore scars and disfigurements of mistreatment. From that dimly remembered course in tropical medicine at St. Louis, I was able to

34

recognize symptoms that said I had lots of work cut out for me.

The sailors had been told not to have too much contact with the refugees because of the contagiousness of their multiple diseases. But, when dealing with bluejackets, you are dealing not with creatures of cold logic but with boys of emotion and charity. Many of them spent hours in the nauseous holds trying to ease the anxieties of Vietnamese minds and the ache of Vietnamese bodies.

I held almost continuous sick-call, aided by my few medical corpsmen and by a rough-handed contingent of pipefitters, boiler tenders and machinist mates "sworn in" for the occasion. Most of those boys knew the sick-bay only as a place where a skillfully feigned bellyache might get a man excused from duty. Yet, with a minimum of instruction, they were soon performing like veterans, passing out pills, cleaning the repulsive ulcers of yaws and slapping on ointments—sometimes the right ones. And never once upchucking or showing any emotion less fitting than heartfelt sympathy.

For the children, milk was distributed by some of the biggest and toughest sailors aboard. These "Milk Maidens," as we called them, had to be big and tough because when they walked into the holds with huge kettles of milk they would be almost stampeded by clamoring masses of child refugees.

For the newborn babies, bottles were needed. From strange, well-hidden places beer bottles appeared with rubber nipples attached. The nipples came from air hoses in the engineroom. They took care of the kids who couldn't guzzle from paper cups.

One of my corpsmen told me about in child in No. 5 hold who seemed to be dying of fulminating diarrhea. The kid was dead before I could confirm my suspicion that he had the disease we still mention only in a whisper—cholera.

To play safe, we insisted upon immediate burial at sea, and that precipitated a near-riot. The boy's relatives all tried to jump overboard after the body. It took several strong-armed sailors to restrain them. We at last were able to coax them to drink some tea, and soon they were slumbering peacefully on the deck. I had dosed that tea with chloral hydrate.

One group of sailors had the unpleasant detail of trying to urge refugees to carry overflowing honey buckets topside and dump them overboard—on the leeward side, of course. These boys also had an unofficial title, but it would never pass the censor.

Now I was seeing for the first time diseases that had been mere names to me. On the first day I isolated ten cases of smallpox. I saw yaws, leprosy, elephantiasis, skin syphilis and, of course, plenty of malaria.

The right to complain is a firmly established and staunchly defended tradition in the United States Navy. But on the *Montague* there were very few complaints from the crew, who had to endure the stench, the shortage of drinking water, the obstacle course on the decks, the extra watches and lookouts and details.

During the night, in order to persuade the children to come topside to the latrines instead of using the decks of the holds, the men on watch would let them carry flashlights. This thrilled the kids and I am sure that many a boy and girl made night visits far beyond the true call of nature.

On some of the lower-deck levels there were areas used as sleeping quarters by the crew. The refugees were supposed to be kept out of these areas but one compartment in particular fascinated the Vietnamese and they could not stay away from it. It was that funny room, with all the shining porcelain bowls in little booths and the higher basins and the long clean white troughs with water running in them all the time. (Of course, occasionally a sailor could be seen relieving himself there, which the refugees were sure that he shouldn't be doing.) Nevertheless, undaunted mothers would sneak into this white room from time to time to wash their babies in the troughs, so handy, so neat. Perhaps a letter of appreciation should be written thanking the Chinal Urinal Company for the excellent baby bathtubs installed on Navy ships.

We not only introduced the Vietnamese to our porcelain facilities; we introduced them to another American institution as well—the beauty contest. On the evening of the second day a contest was held and a refugee girl chosen as best-looking of the lot was crowned Miss Passage to Freedom. She was selected by the Captain, dressed in a surgical robe from sick bay, and given a crown fashioned by the boys in the radio shack. She sat on a throne built in the carpenter shop and was awarded an extra ration of fruit by the cooks. All this delighted her and she rewarded us with black-toothed, betel-stained smiles.

There was a French liaison officer on each ship and a control team who translated from Vietnamese into French and sometimes into English. They traveled back and forth and were considered part of the crew. Over loud speakers, they explained the strange American habits to the refugees: "Urinals are for urinating, latrines are for latrining and, fear not, the babies will not be eaten alive by the sailors."

The refugees had seen a Communist pamphlet with a picture of a Navy doctor, not unlike Dooley, vaccinating people with deadly germs. But the prize, I think, was a drawing of an LCT (amphibious landing craft) that carried its passengers far out to sea, then opened its giant maw and spewed them overboard.

Now the mandarins shook their heads solemnly over the enormity of such lies and apologized for the people's having believed them. They promised to work diligently to dispel groundless fears. But already a more powerful corrective was working on the people's hearts and minds.

By this time many of the refugees were watching our sailors with bug-eyed wonder. On the faces of the children there was a certain softening that might even be laughter. And why not? I have never seen anything funnier—or more inspiring—than red-necked American sailors seriously performing the duties of baby-sitters and maids-of-all-work.

Other strange things began to happen on the *Montague*.

Loaves of bread, enormous quantities of candy, cigarettes, soft drinks and other articles were appearing in the hands of the old and the young. It was not theft—unless a sailor purloining something to slip to his new Tonkinese friends be stealing. I saw one notoriously loud, cursing boatswain's mate on the forecastle, bouncing a brown bare-bottom baby on his knee while stuffing a Baby Ruth into its toothless mouth. It would have pleased their mothers, as it pleased me, to see their sailor sons caring for this shipload.

Throughout the ship, these little acts of spontaneous kindness were happening by the hundreds, and none of them was lost on our fearful and suspicious refugees. This was the force, heartfelt and uncontrived, that finally washed away the poisons of Communist hatred.

On each of the three mornings we were enroute, a priest offered Mass in the various holds. It was poignant to hear these weary, bedraggled exiles, singing softly their thanks to God, who seemed temporarily to be looking away from them. Yet their faith was strong and comforting and made us humble in their presence. I noticed that the sailors, working on deck with unusual quietness, always listened to the services.

Dawn of the third day found the *Montague* at the mouth of the Saigon River, where the pilot came aboard. After three hours, the ship would arrive at the capital of South Viet Nam, Saigon.

There, at the debarkation pier, the refugees were unloaded from the vessel which in so short a time had won their love. By this time the sailors were not monsters but

39

"Tot Lam," or "Very nice." The old man who three days before had shrunk from the touch of an American sailor now smiled with his eyes at one who was helping him alight. Both were smoking a Lucky. Many of the children clung to their favorite sailors to the last moment, and several of them went off waving trophies.

Nevertheless, when they left there must have been a feeling of relief in the refugees' hearts and a similar feeling was evident on the sailors' faces. The mass of suckling infants and lively youngsters were gone. The adults who had been sprawling over the decks were gone. But odors of fish, oriental spices and human offal remained. Tied up just behind our AKA was the French luxury liner, *La Marseillaise*. How incongruous it seemed with its decks so clean and white while ours were matted with filth.

At the pier we were met by representatives of the Military Assistance Advisory Group, the American mission assisting in the relocation of the newly arrived refugees. This was my introduction to MAAG and a traumatic one at that.

I was at the bottom of the gangway trying to get some of the coolie-types who were standing around the dock to help the refugees with their bundles. But I wasn't getting anywhere. A tall, lanky, lean, dyspeptic-looking Lieutenant Colonel ambled up to my side and mumbled: "Take it easy, Lieutenant, they won't hurry; it's siesta time." This raised my Irish wrath and, as a consequence, the Navy shouted at the Army and the Army reciprocated. All this afforded the refugees a great show. Later I was properly introduced to Lieutenant Colonel Erwin Jones of the MAAG office in Saigon, a slow-talking, hot-tempered Georgia rebel. Oddly enough our dockside clash led to a relationship which I will always cherish. Erv Jones is now my very good friend, and his presence in Indo-China during that troubled year was decidedly a help.

Just before the debarkation of the refugees was completed, Bishop Pietro Martino Ngô-dinh-Thûc, Vicar Apostolic of Vinh-Long, who was in Saigon, paid a visit to our ship. He is the brother of the defiant Prime Minister, Ngo Dinh Diem, a man who never bowed to the French and who stated emphatically that the Geneva partitioning of Indo-China would lead to a new and more murderous war. The Bishop blessed the refugees and in the name of the Vietnamese Government thanked the officers and the crew of the *Montague* for their mission. He begged God and man to clean the world of its sorrows and blood and despair.

As the refugees filed off, each was given a paper bag with two pounds of rice and two packages of cigarettes, all tagged with the name of our ship and our mission's title, "Passage to Freedom." There were large open trucks at the pier which transported the people to the resettlement areas then under construction, thanks to American Aid.

After the debarkation the ship was given a direly needed clean-up. Clamoring over the side came a gang of coolies MAAG had scraped up. Under the direction of the sailors they manned salt-water hoses and washed the ships fore and aft as thoroughly as possible. Then at 1600 came Liberty Call—relief from shipboard duties and freedom

41

to go ashore in Saigon, the Paris of the East. It was a Cinderella liberty; we had orders to return to the ship by midnight.

In spite of the anaesthetic effect of good French alcohol, on our return we found that the peculiar musty human odor remained.

Captain Cox posted the official record of the voyage. We had transported 2,061 people. There had been two deaths, two burials at sea. Doctor Dooley had officiated at four births, mothers and babies all doing well—including one little guy who faces life bearing the burden of a name dreamed up by his proud parents, Think Van AKA Montague 98 Ngham.

Before turning in, I stood on the deck congratulating myself on being a Navy doctor. "Dooley," I said to myself, "you've seen and done things that are out of this world—but you'll never have another experience to top this one in your whole lifetime."

That's what *I* thought.

CHAPTER V

DR. AMBERSON'S TEAM

We returned to Haiphong, picked up another load of refugees, and made another round-trip, which was to be the last of my "cargo runs." By now the anchorage in the Baie d'Along was filled with ships—four APAs (troop transports) and three more AKAs like our own.

The *Montague* was now famous. We had the best health and sanitation record. We were equipped with the biggest and best latrines, the most massive chow lines, the stoutest ladders, and the most mammoth waste-disposal unit. All the other ships were designing and building their own facilities for the evacuation, so our advice was much in demand.

One day I was invited aboard a newly-arrived transport to give a medical and sanitation briefing. While on deck I heard the ship's captain yelling orders in English to a French landing-craft alongside. The French crew obviously knew no English and the situation was beautifully fouled up. I speak French fluently so I decided to go up on the bridge and make myself useful.

43

The skipper glared at me and said, "Later, doctor!"

I cleared my throat. "Beg pardon, sir, but——"

"I told you—later!"

"Captain," I said quietly, "I speak French. I thought I might help."

"Hell's bells, why didn't you say so?" he roared. "Tell that idiot to pull away and come alongside Chinese-fashion."

I shouted the orders in French, and the landing-craft came around smoothly with its bow to the transport's stern. I got a grateful salute from the Frenchman and a gruff "Thank-you" from the skipper. But as I left the bridge I noticed the predatory look in his eye.

That started it. Word got around that young Dooley could speak French, an advantage not to be overlooked in dealing with the people of a French colony. Soon I was performing all sorts of extra duties that had nothing to do with the practice of medicine.

It was at this time that the flagship of Rear Admiral Lorenzo S. Sabin pulled into the bay. The Admiral was in command of Task Force 90, to whom this evacuation task had fallen. In the rough months to come, I would often invoke his name and authority, sometimes a little recklessly, to get things done. But I did not meet the Admiral until close to the wind-up of the new operation on which I was to be engaged. Then I was to learn that he had been aware of my unorthodox conduct and had given me unreserved support.

I was ordered now to report aboard the flagship to the

Force Medical Officer, Captain James Grindell, Medical Corps, U. S. Navy. He told me that he was going to organize a Preventive Medicine and Sanitation Unit in the port city of Haiphong. Later I learned that Admiral Sabin had requested permission from the French to send a party of 1,800 men ashore to build reception-centers. He was allowed to send only 18. The place was inundated with refugees and would soon be infested with all sorts of diseases, including the fancier tropical varieties. The local population would be exposed to plagues and epidemics, and there was a strong possibility that the diseases would spread to American crews aboard the evacuation ships and also to Saigon, where we were depositing our uprooted humanity.

Then Captain Grindell laid it on the line.

"Doctor," he said, "I am considering attaching you to this unit as a medical officer and—well, as a sort of interpreter, let's say. You understand, of course, that this is a voluntary duty. Strictly voluntary. So make up your own mind."

When a man with four gold stripes on his arm, and speaking for the Admiral, says that he is considering a junior lieutenant for something, well, the job is as good as done. Of course, I volunteered. And that is how I became part of the shore-based medical and sanitation unit that soon dwindled into Operation Cockroach under my command.

I hated to leave the *Montague*. It had been my own ship for the past month. Its officers and crew were a great lot of guys, genuine and good. I felt a strong bond to the sailors

45

who had obeyed my slave-driving orders while performing all the loathsome details of the first passage. I never knew what they thought of Dooley until the night we said goodbye.

Then they surprised me with a little ceremony on deck. Traditionally, the *Montague's* enlisted men select from among their own company a Shipmate of the Month. He is given a scroll and his name is listed in the ship's archives. The crew elected me as the Shipmate of the Month and I was the only officer they had ever selected. Having served my hitch as an enlisted man, I could appreciate better than most officers the unusual nature of this tribute, and I had a hard time controlling the tears that come so easily to an Irishman's eyes. If my luck holds out, I may collect other honors in the course of my Navy career. But none can ever occupy quite the same spot in my heart as the honor bestowed upon me by the men of the *Montague*. During the presentation all I could think of was how many times I had raised hell with the men as I ordered them into unappetizing sanitation details, how I had shouted at many, and become angry with a few.

In official theory I was on permanent station duty at the Naval Hospital in Yokosuka, Japan, just loaned to the *Montague* on TAD. The arrangement seems favored in the Far East. It keeps ships supplied with medical service without tying one man down to long-term duty on relatively small ships.

When Captain Grindell decided that I would be sent to the newly formed Preventive Medicine Unit in Haiphong, it involved a lot of administrative red-tape. However, it was worked out without too much sweat; in fact, Captain "Rusty" Ball, the Commanding Officer of my hospital in Japan did not seem to express any particular interest in getting me back. For the first but not the last time, my TAD orders were extended, this time for an additional three months.

On the *Estes*, Admiral Sabin's flagship, I met the officers of the newly minted PMS unit: Captain Julius Amberson, a distinguished medical officer, who would be in command; Lt. Comdr. Edmund Gleason from the Medical Service Corps who knows more about hygiene and sanitation than any contender of his weight; Lt. Richard Kaufman of the Fleet Epidemological Control Unit, and Lt. David Davis, another doctor, who would be with us for less than fifteen days. Captain Amberson had brought along a dozen enlisted men from Korea and Dick Kaufman had a staff of laboratory technicians in tow. Ed Gleason and Dooley were strictly on their own.

Captain Grindell read the mission's orders: "To prevent epidemics in our personnel, and to provide humanitarian care and medical attention for the refugees as they come within the orbit of our operations." At the time I wondered if we weren't a rather small company for such an ambitious undertaking. But even if I hadn't been as green as I was, I couldn't have foreseen the shape of things to come.

"All right, gentlemen, that's it," Captain Grindell con-

47

cluded. "Lots of luck to you." The meeting stood adjourned.

And now a word about Doctor Amberson. In all the branches of the service one will meet individuals to whom a cross-eyed baboon would not want to claim relationship. But you also meet men of the moral and intellectual caliber of Dr. Amberson. He was a superb leader and had a wonderful quality of immediately winning the loyalty of all who worked for, or rather, as he would say, with him. He was one of the most honestly patriotic men I have ever met. He had that important command ability to delegate his authority when he deemed it necessary. Dr. Amberson, whether he knows it or not (and I don't believe he does), was one reason why I chose the regular Navy for my career. To work for men like him, men who know and practice the lofty qualities cited in every officer's commission, will always be a pleasure and an honorable duty.

We left the *Estes* one afternoon, took a trip ashore in an open boat and hitched a ride into Haiphong. There a French truck drove us to the best hotel, which was damned miserable—Gleason to perform miracles of sanitation; Kaufman to comb fleas from rats and beg stool specimens from astonished refugees; and Captain Amberson to command and also to stiffen the spine of a junior lieutenant who still didn't realize the "humanitarian care and medical attention" of half a million or so refugees was soon to be his responsibility alone.

CHAPTER VI

THE CITY OF HAIPHONG

At the mouth of the delta on the Gulf of Tonkin, only about 100 miles from the southern frontier of the Chinese province of Kwangsi, Haiphong rates as the best port south of Hong Kong. Yet even in its best days Haiphong was a city of slums, muck and squalor, a rat-infested city inured to swarms of flies and clouds of mosquitoes.

Most large seaport towns have a definite pattern. There are business areas with buildings ranging from skyscrapers on down. There are residential areas and the lowest fringe is usually the waterfront, home of thugs, juvenile delinquents, blaring juke boxes and flop houses. So it is in New York, Marseilles, Saigon and elsewhere.

It was not so in Haiphong. There the docks were almost beautiful, large, built out over the water, wide and sturdy. On the other side of the railroad tracks which ran within a few feet of the piers, there were warehouses, each large enough to house a baseball field. These were built of concrete and had swinging doors wide enough to accommodate

49

three trucks driven abreast. Next came rows of roomy supply depots with huge storage areas, some of them under tin roofs. All this was to be a rich plum for the hungry Communists in less than a year.

The first two or three blocks beyond the piers had some gracious homes, requisitioned during my stay there by the French High Command, consisting of General René Cogny and his staff. There were parks, complete with fountains, statues and the inevitable pigeons.

The Governor's palace, a pink stucco mansion three stories high, stood just beyond the docks, along with the City Hall and the Mayor's residence. These buildings had broad lawns and majestic mahogany trees. Beyond this point the city rapidly deteriorated.

The main street, Rue Paul Bert, ran parallel to the docks, four blocks away. Everything beyond was squalor. Here were the slums, bazaars, flea market, native quarters, Indian quarters, delapidated pagodas, grimy river waterways, fifth-hand shopping districts, the city jail and, in an adjoining building, the city hospital.

The French Naval Base, on the harbor, was composed of several good-sized buildings and dozens of American-made Quonset huts. Admiral Jean Marie Querville, the French Navy's Commanding Officer during the evacuation of the Tonkin, managed to dismantle a good deal of the base. All the Quonset huts were taken down and shipped south, everything was removed that could be removed without violating clauses of the treaty relating to the destruction of permanent buildings. On many of the buildings the letters "MF" (Marine Francaise) were emblazoned into the concrete facades. Admiral Querville had them chipped out before the buildings were turned over to the Communist Viet Minh.

Neither of the city's two hotels, the Continental and the Paris, had American-type plumbing or running water. But both had the largest cockroaches and rats I have ever seen. When you stepped toward the cockroaches, instead of running away, they ran *toward* you. The rats were large enough to saddle, and they loved to fight.

The rooms were big, with ancient beds under mosquito netting and a couple of aged, musty, velvet-covered chairs. There was a small dance hall on the first of my hotel's two floors, and the cheap music sounded until midnight. It boasted some taxi girls that you could rent for a dance, or for a few hours. Such dance halls were the only places in town, save for a few bawdy bars, that played Western music for the entertainment of the French troops. By Western I mean not Eastern.

We Americans lived for awhile in the Paris and then moved to the Continental. When the others left in October, I stayed on there alone. After a few weeks, I knew every song the orchestra played and I knew what time it was by listening. When "Blues in the Night" started, it was 9:30. At 10:00 it was "Tea for Two." At 11:30 "Love for Sale" was the tops on the pops. The shop always closed with a stirring rendition of the "Marseillaise."

The main street and some of the side streets had the Indian stores to be found all over the Orient. Here one could

51

buy spices, French perfume, cheap woolens and cheaper silks. There were a few good but dirty restaurants where you could buy Indian curry so hot that you did not dare to light a cigarette after you ate for fear of blowing up.

In the early months of the evacuation, French wines and canned foods were available at the military cooperatives. They did not last long, however, as the French were evacuating their military forces as fast as possible. During the last few months, no western foods or wines or even bottled waters were available anywhere in the Tonkin.

The shoeshine boys, who roamed the streets like herds of small cattle, were one pleasant facet of the city to me. They were just little tramps—accomplished thieves—but they were good little tramps and good thieves. They shined my rough combat boots—the inside-out leather type. They rubbed and spat and grinned, and did it again. I would ask them, "Ong di nam Viet khomp?" "Are you going to become a refugee and leave this Communist land?" It was the first expression I learned in Vietnamese. "Yes," they would reply, "we are going south, sometime."

These kids couldn't quite get out the absurd word "Dooley." They called me "Bac Sy My," which, I soon discovered, meant "American Naval Doctor." Later on, when our work got more involved, the kids became a good junior intelligence network. Someone once called them "little Dooleys." I was flattered.

The part of Haiphong that I loved most was really the worst. It was that squirming Oriental bazaar—a real one, not a Cecil B. De Mille reproduction. The bazaar covered an enormous square on one side of the Rue Paul Bert.

Normally the population of Haiphong was about 100,000, but when we arrived in August, 1954 it had been doubled at least by the grey tides of refugees sweeping into the city. With baskets and bundles, they sprawled in the streets, gutters and alleys around the bazaar, and covered the parks like swarming ant-heaps. Through this filth and confusion moved detachments of French sailors and Foreign Legionnaires, busily evacuating French military and civilian property from the doomed city.

Around the fringes of the bazaar were the less revolting displays—fruit, flowers, vegetables, tennis shoes, stolen cameras and binoculars; but deep in the dark recesses, under straw roofs, were the stalls selling rancid butter and fish oils, flyblown pastries and pies, nauseating soft drinks, native beer designed to take a coat from the lining of your stomach, and red meat that could be seen only when the vendor waved away the solid covering of black flies.

Other meats—including cows' heads, birds' eyes, bat wings, dog entrails, dried cockroaches—was dispensed on knee-high platforms. The medicine stall displayed big glass jars of water in which snakes had been allowed to decay; taken daily, with a side-dose of dog liver, this was an all-purpose Tonkinese wonder drug.

Everywhere was the sharp, staccato sound of dried mahogany sticks clapped together. It meant soup for sale. Children wielded the sticks, while their parents sat over

53

blackened pots incessantly stirring the half-congealed
brews. Fat yellow dogs and sickly infants with the shining
potbellies of famine wandered through the din.

Vegetables? You could buy mouldy potatoes, bright car-
rots, lettuce, watercress and fantastically large radishes, all
guaranteed to give a Western stomach a good case of
worms. Tuberculosis milk (from cows, goats and humans)
—very cheap this week. And there were areas inside the
bazaar where the sun never shone. There you could buy
"nuoc mom," the chili sauce of the Orient, the oil from
decaying fish mixed with salt. That was the stuff I had
ordered thrown overboard that first day on the *Montague.*

While walking you were softly slugged with the heavy
hanging cloud of caramel fragrance, sweet opium, drifting
hashish. The mournful chants of beggars clashed with the
shrieking of children, the shrill cries of hawkers and shoppers, the haggling and barking and bickering. Everything
pushed, swayed, moved and, above all, smelled.

Women were bent double, with babies strapped to their
backs, and there were others with bellies heavy with their
unborn. There were women with their hair meticulously
wrapped around their heads and perfumed with oil, carrying children whose hair was covered with a cradle cap and
secondarily scabbed with pus. Abruptly one broke out into
the daylight on the other side of this Oriental emporium.
Here was another flower market, in all its beauty, a heaven
next to a hell. There was a spot on the corner that would
sell the things that are used in the Buddhist pagodas—

paper idols, multi-colored dolls and animals, and slow-burning, sweet-smelling joss sticks. There were constant mournful chants from the mouths of the beggars, the shrieking of the children, the shrill cries of the women, the hawkers and the shoppers.

This was Haiphong, my home until the middle of the following May.

In front of most native homes, whether hovels or mansions, there were usually small red ribbons of paper with drawings of grimacing faces on them. There was an old legend about two brothers who could spot demons even in daylight and could frighten them away. Heaven therefore gave them the mission of barring the way of evil spirits, which were so terrified of the brothers that even their faces on red paper sent them flying.

Perhaps the people of Viet Nam should have hung these wonder-working ribbons all around their country. Then the legendary brothers might have barred the way to the demons of Communism stalking outside, and now holding the upper half of the country in their strangling grip.

Looking at the refugee-overrun city of Haiphong, one did not need to be a doctor to recognize that it was rotten ripe for the outbreak of typhus, smallpox, cholera and other plagues. We said little about it; words were unnecessary.

Depending on your nature, you either yielded to a sense of helplessness or you plunged into work, to reduce the suffering even a little and so help save an edge of dignity for Man—who is supposed to be only a little lower than the angels.

We did not have a single epidemic in Haiphong, in our camps outside the city or on our naval transports, in the entire period of the evacuation. That was to be the final measure of our work.

CHAPTER VII

HOW DID IT ALL COME ABOUT?

Now that this was to be my new job, I wanted to find out a little about its background. I understood that the three countries of Laos, Cambodia and Viet Nam combined to make up Indo-China, richest colony of France. I also vaguely remembered that it was the Emperor of Laos who offered President Truman a division of Combat Elephants to help the war effort in Korea.

Doctor Amberson was able to assist me with some general background material; Ed Gleason, Dave Davis and Dick Kaufman didn't know much more than I did. But we learned.

After eight years of war, the Geneva treaty, signed six weeks earlier, had divided Viet Nam at the 17th Parallel into two "temporary zones of political influence" until things could be settled by a national plebiscite in July 1956. Viet Nam herself, the country which was divided, did not even sign the treaty which divided her. Meanwhile her southern half, with a population of 11 million, was to be

57

ruled by the National government in Saigon, and the Northern half, with a population of 10 million, was to be controlled by the Viet Minh Communists under the leadership of Ho Chi Minh.

An important clause in the cease-fire agreement provided that a crescent-shaped area around Haiphong was to remain an "open zone to both parties." This was to serve as a staging area for the evacuation of those people in the north who preferred exile in South Viet Nam to life under the Communists. The agreement was that these people were not only to be *allowed* but *assisted* to move south; and a mixed neutral commission, composed of representatives of Canada, Poland and India, was created to supervise the evacuation.

But this small "open zone" around Haiphong was scheduled to shrink gradually, and on specified dates, until in the middle of May 1955 the entire area, including the city of Haiphong, would be given to the Communists. Obviously this was a tricky agreement—just how tricky we would soon learn.

But why were the French so hated by the natives? And what had France done here that was good and had won her continuing American support? I wrote home and asked a friend to send me some books on this baffling country. It will suggest how confusing the subject was to the average American if I tell you that he sent to Indo-China a book entitled "Problems of Indonesia."

After some weeks I felt that I had at least a slight grasp

on the situation, so I wrote it all down, with carbons, for anyone who might be interested.

Viet Nam is located in the highly strategic area of southeast Asia. She lies directly south of China, whose province of Kwangsi is less than a hundred miles north of Haiphong. The China Sea washes Viet Nam's east coast and on the western border is the Kingdom of Laos with its elephants and tigers. The southwest border is formed by the equally ancient kingdom of Cambodia, one of the most rapidly developing nations of Asia.

Japan conquered Viet Nam in 1940. Within three months, by using Viet Nam's raw materials, airfields and seaports, Japan was able to overthrow Cambodia, Laos, Formosa, Thailand, Burma, Indonesia and Malaya. She became a threat to Australia and marched to the very gates of India.

Utilizing such seaports as Haiphong and Saigon, Japan shipped weapons and materials east which led to the defeat of MacArthur's forces and the conquest of the Philippines in 1942.

Economically, Viet Nam is important as the world's fourth largest producer of natural rubber. Her two deltas of the Tonkin in the north and the Cochin in the south produce a rich surplus of exportable rice. Her mountains abound in ores.

In the eighteenth and nineteenth centuries, Europe discovered the wealth of the Orient and all too eagerly shouldered the "white man's burden." England mastered the subcontinent of India. Holland seized the Pacific islands now called Indonesia, the Dutch East Indies. And France, in the 1860's and 1870's, achieved dominion over the three fabulous, story-book kingdoms of Indo-China. From then, until August 1954, Indo-China was a colony of France.

France did many fine things in Indo-China. She brought in the first rubber tree. She developed mines and minerals and built a system of roadways and waterways. Thousands of French families settled in the colony permanently, coming to think of it as their rightful home.

But France did not put into Viet Nam the equivalent of what she took out. She had a political and economic stake in keeping the native masses backward, submissive and ignorant of the arts of government. In a nation of 23-odd million, she built only one university. She was no more selfish than other colonial powers. She was simply following the patterns of the period.

In 1940, France yielded Indo-China to Japan without a real struggle. She set up a provisional government to protect her interests and managed to do "business as usual" with the invaders. It is ironic to note that an important member of that provisional government, Jean Sainteny, at this writing is in the Red capital of Hanoi as head of a French mission seeking to do "business as usual" with the Communist Viet Minh.

In 1945 Viet Nam, Laos and Cambodia were liberated, not by the French, but by the English and Americans.

At this time a man who had become well-known and beloved in the underground during the Japanese occupation came into additional prominence. He would say: "We

60

have gained our independence from the Japanese and I see no reason why we should again yield it to France. We are a strong nation and we will be our own rulers." He set himself up in Hanoi as the president of the "Democratic Republic of Viet Nam." He was Ho Chi Minh, which means Ho, the Enlightened One.

The French sent Ho Chi Minh into exile but on December 19, 1946, his forces started a war for independence— started it by disemboweling more than 1000 native women in Hanoi because they had been working for, married to, or living with the French.

Many Americans, though they shuddered at such obscene methods, sympathized with his ultimate goals, considering him a patriotic Vietnamese Nationalist. Such nationalists were winning the struggle with colonial powers all over Asia.

During this time, I was a student in college in Paris and I can remember the campaigns for collections of clothes and money to send to the forces of Ho Chi Minh, now called the Viet Minh. I can recall contributing a few dollars to this organization.

But in 1949, after the Communists had conquered China, Ho showed his true colors by proclaiming the Democratic Republic of Viet Nam—which was promptly recognized by the U.S.S.R., Communist China, and other satellite states of the Soviet bloc. Ho Chi Minh had been a Moscow-trained puppet from the start.

After 1949, the United States supplied military and economic aid in the struggle to save Viet Nam from the

61

Communists. But again we failed to make our objectives clear to the people. After the fall of Dien Bien Phu and the tragedy at Geneva, there were Vietnamese who hated the Viet Minh and the French with equal fervor, but who hated the Americans too because the French had fought with American aid. So again the job of winning friends and influencing people was left to a few men in uniform who, officially, had other fish to fry.

However, to the rice-paddy-worker and the coolie there was no difference between 1948 and 1950. One could not speak to such men of dialectical materialism and the new Red imperialism. They had no grasp of the complexities of Communism because these concepts related to nothing within their own traditions or experiences. The rice-paddy-worker knew only that the underground hero and his soldiers, many of them from their own villages, were fighting and often defeating the French. To him this was "Viet Minh Nationalism." He did not know he was placing himself in the bondage of Communism; he only wanted to be free of the yoke of colonialism.

Only when and where the Viet Minh took and held power did the people begin to savor the abstraction called Communism, and for the most part they did not relish the flavor. Slowly, under beguiling slogans and promises, the new masters were taking away their lands, undermining the family loyalty of their children, conscripting their bodies and—especially for the two million Christians— outraging their souls.

And so the war continued until 1954. It did not directly

affect Americans living in Kansas City and Decatur and Jacksonville. However, when the battle of Dien Bien Phu began, the eyes of the world focussed on this far-away post. This was our awakening.

By the time the complex struggle came to a head at Dien Bien Phu, the free world no longer had any illusions. It was aware that the life-and-death interests of Washington and London were at stake on one side as surely as those of Moscow and Peiping were on the other. Catastrophe stalked the Tonkin.

Many of us remember Dien Bien Phu, remember how fifteen thousand men fought there. We remember that the number of French dead was fantastic and that most of them died knowing that the fortress was doomed but continuing to fight nonetheless, for the honor of France.

Dien Bien Phu really marked the end of the war in Indo-China. That isolated outpost fell to the Viet Minh in May, 1954. On July 21st of the same year the Treaty of Geneva was signed and officially ended the war. Secretary of State John Foster Dulles walked out of that conference saying that the United States would not sign the treaty because we would not be a party to an agreement that handed over half a country to totalitarian tyranny.

Geneva's promises were many. Most important was the clause that said that the country of Viet Nam was to be divided into two "zones of political influence." The one north of the 17th parallel, the large Tonkin delta with 10 million people would be given to the Viet Minh, the Communist government of Ho Chi Minh; the 11 million people south of the 17th parallel would live under the rule of Premier, now President, Ngo Dinh Diem.

The second important clause stated that anyone living in one zone who wished to go to the other would be allowed to make, and aided in making, this transfer. If they were in the Tonkin of the north and wished to go south, they were to proceed to the port city of Haiphong, where ships would transport them. The small crescent-shaped area around Hanoi and Haiphong was to remain "free" until May 19, 1955. This area was to shrink on successive dates. On May 19, 1955 all the area north of the 17th parallel would be handed over to the Viet Minh.

Early in August there was a trickle of refugees into Hanoi and Haiphong, which are about forty miles apart. In that same month, Vietnamese and French officials asked the U.S. to assist their own forces to evacuate from the Tonkin all the refugees who might want to leave. The United States instantly agreed, Task Force 90 received its orders and within a few days the great exodus was in swing. Neither the French nor the Communists, least of all the Americans, could foresee that it would assume the dimensions it did. In Viet Nam a proud and noble race paid a staggering price in human misery for the issues of freedom. The deal was closed now; Viet Nam had not won.

That was the background as we settled down in the musty, dusty Hotels Paris and Continental.

CHAPTER VIII

CAMP DE LA PAGODE

Through years of college and medical school I had taken courses in everything from Aristotle to Zoology. Unhappily none of this education included a course in refugee camp building. Dr. Amberson did not indicate that he was aware of this gap in my store of knowledge.

It was obvious that the first problem we would have with the refugees would be that of housing. There were perhaps 150,000 living in the most squalid conditions, sprawling out over the city streets and gutters. There was no sanitation of any kind. The refugees were living under shelters improvised from rice mats, cloth or plastic rain covers.

On our second day in Haiphong, Captain Amberson tossed a sheaf of notes and sketches at me. "Dooley," he said, "your job will be to build refugee camps. There's the general idea. Now get going. And don't bother me about the details." Aye, aye, sir. But at that moment I didn't know the difference between a refugee camp and a playground for girls.

65

You can't build a refugee camp in the middle of a city; therefore, we looked around on the outskirts. Most of the outskirts consisted of rice paddies or bogs along the edges of the Red River. Finally we found a reasonably dry spot about four miles from town, on the road leading from Hanoi into Haiphong. "Highway" in Viet Nam describes a barely navigable dirt road. At this time, the site was about 40 miles from the Bamboo Curtain, which gave us a little elbow-room. By October 11, under the Geneva schedule, the town of Haiduong would be swallowed, bringing the outposts of Communism within fifteen miles of us, and in January the Curtain would be visible from the camp itself.

Many unkind things have been said about how slowly the cogs of American agencies move. Yet within a few days after he had been informed of our plans, Mike Adler, head of the U.S. Foreign Operations Administration (USOM) in Haiphong, had 400 large tents flown in from Japan. "Army Sixty-Man Tents" they were called; for us they often sheltered 120 people or more.

To help us set up the tents the French Union Forces furnished us some Moroccan soldiers and we found a few hundred coolies. The design of the camp was there in Dr. Amberson's sketch. He was the brain and we were his hands. I was learning how to build tent camps.

After several days of work, the first camp was completed. The tents were arranged in twelve rows. All told, we erected 149 tents, with a broad roadway through the middle of the camp. An elaborate set of drainage ditches kept the place from floating away during the monsoon season, though the ditches did form something of an obstacle course. If you didn't walk with one eye on the ground, you were liable to find yourself knee-deep in a ditch.

Certain broad paddies surrounding the camp were used as latrines. I pulled a few prize boners, which Dr. Amberson caught in time, like locating the latrine area on the windward side. One problem required continuous effort on our part—to educate the refugees not to take their soapless baths in the same paddy they were using as a flushless toilet. About once a month we would spray these fields with a strong insecticide solution. This would kill the bugs and throw into spasms any poor refugee who happened to get caught with his pants down when we were spraying.

Later, in some of the other camps, we dug Marine-type slit trenches and straddle trenches to be used as toilets. A circular windbreak was put around them. The refugees always stayed dutifully within the windbreak but were not in the least anxious to use the trenches themselves. My corpsmen, with the ingenuity of enlisted men, gradually moved the windbreak closer and closer to the trenches until the refugees were finally forced to use them; there was nowhere else to go.

One time, in the early months, we borrowed Commodore Walter Winn's helicopter, hovered over the area and dumped DDT powder through a hose in the bottom of the plane. A great deal of it fell to the earth, but an equally large amount blew back up in our faces. The refugees on the ground watched this astonishing procedure and shouted with glee the equivalent of "What bizarre people, these Americans! They have a fixation on excrement and strange white powder." The helicopter-dusting plan went up in a cloud of DDT.

The colony was scarcely a lovely sight to the eyes and certainly no treat to the nose. Nevertheless, we were pleased, even elated. A beginning had been made. The first row of tents I reserved for my hospital area—a tent for sick call, a "nursery" for new-born babies, several supply tents and five or six tents for sick patients. I also set aside tents for the elders or mandarins who would act as camp leaders.

We had one large tent in which we stored rice and straw mats. The rice had a private scent all its own (boll weevils, I believe), while the straw mats had a musty odor, especially in the monsoon season. The canvas had a scent and the pungent insecticides we used had theirs. Corpsmen Baker and Harris had a pet baboon, Jasmine, who made her home in this tent too. Blend all these aromas together and add the draft from the washrooms and you will see why visitors never had any difficulty in locating our headquarters.

We christened our first camp "Refugee Camp de la Pagode." The name seemed Oriental and melodious, despite the fact that the area was fresh out of pagodas.

This was just the first camp. Others were to come: Camp Cement, Camp Shell, Camp Lach Tray, Jardin des Enfants, to mention a few. We were obliged to move fairly frequently, when the mud would no longer support us, or when the Red frontier came uncomfortably close, or in one instance when we were driven out by rats, four-legged variety. Like old circus hands, my meagre staff and volunteer refugees were soon adept in tearing 'em down and putting 'em up.

The Vietnamese Refugee Evacuation Committee of Haiphong was directed by Mr. Mai Van Ham, who became one of my best friends. He gave me everything I asked for, from extra coolies to some insight into the Oriental mind. He was frequently at odds with the French and occasionally with an impatient doctor. Sometimes we almost came to blows, but the situation would always resolve itself when we both realized that, each in his own fashion, we were endeavoring to do our utmost for Viet Nam's oppressed. Mai Van Ham is a true patriot. His tireless devotion to his overwhelming task was magnificent.

Now we began to round up the refugees and move them in with us. In the Medical Tent we held daily sick call. Here, with our American Aid medicines, we saw three to four hundred refugees every day. Respiratory diseases were common, as were trachoma, worm infestations, fungus infections, tinea and tuberculosis. These were just everyday run-of-the-mill complaints. Every corpsman I ever had could soon identify a case of yaws at ten feet.

The Navy supplied our unit with every piece of machinery, a truck, water tanks, a jeep and insecticides. However, it didn't seem quite fair to the Navy that we should ask it, officially, for soap, vitamin pills, dressings and aspirin for the hundreds of thousands of people who eventually were to pass through our area.

During the months of August through October, we acquired most of our pharmacy for the camp's sick-call through that time-honored, slightly illegitimate, Oriental custom known as cumshaw. My corpsmen and I would take turns running out to the bay in boats or hitch-hiking on the Commodore's helicopter. Any nearby U.S. ship was our target. We would bum a dozen bottles of vitamins, half a dozen vials of penicillin, a handful of band-aids, some antibiotics, a few hemostats—we would accept anything they were willing to give. Through the unbounded generosity of the Navy, unbeknownst to the Navy, we amassed a formidable armamentarium of drugs.

In return for these gifts to cumshaw we would give lectures to the crews on just what was happening and describe what most of the refugees had to endure to escape. We often carried a large plastic-covered map of French Indo-China with us to dramatize the 17th parallel. The talks were always well received.

And so, through this quasi-honorable means, we kept our pharmacy stocked. However, by December most of the ships had left and only four or five transports remained. We couldn't keep going back to them, so we devised another system.

I decided to write home for medicines. Terramycin was the most important drug, so I wrote first to the Pfizer Laboratories Division of Charles Pfizer and Company, Brooklyn, N. Y. I told them of our job, of our people, our camp and our problems. I even sent some photos. My letter closed with a request for a "small contribution—of, say, 25,000 capsules—of terramycin."

The Pfizer Company responded immediately with 50,000 capsules. Later they sent some penicillin, streptomycin, and magnamycin. The total commercial value must have been tens of thousands of dollars. Its real value to us was incalculable.

In response to my letter, Meade-Johnson of Evansville, Indiana, sent us many gallons of liquid vitamin preparation; Pan American Airways sent 10,000 bars of soap, and other companies sent many other things. This was the "decadent capitalistic system of America" responding.

Rest assured, we continually explained to thousands of refugees, as individuals and in groups, that only in a country which permits companies to grow large could such fabulous charity be found. With every one of the thousands of capsules of terramycin and with every dose of vitamins on a baby's tongue, these words were said: "Dai La My-Quoc Vien-Tro" (This is American Aid).

These companies performed a great service; I am sure not their first. They didn't send regrets, they didn't promise to "investigate" my claim; they responded with the enthusiasm of great corporations in a great country. When I wrote to thank them, telling them of the impact their contributions had made, they responded with letters thanking *me*. Imagine that! Every person from whom I requested aid responded wholeheartedly. It gave me a feeling of nearness to all the people in my country. It was as if all

71

the wealth of America were in my own medicine chest. All
I had to do was reach and ask, and reach and ask I did.
Camp de la Pagode became a corner drugstore. About all
we lacked were comic books and ice cream.

Mike Adler had a small warehouse of medicines flown
up from U.S.O.M. supplies. These were sent to the Viet
Nam Public Health Office in Haiphong, which in turn sent
them to us—always with a smile. It was American Aid
reversing itself. "From U.S.O.M. to Viet Nam to the American doctor."

At Camp de la Pagode we processed potable water. Our
aim was a gallon per refugee per day and sometimes, daily,
this was as much as 12,000 gallons. If medals could be
awarded to machines, I would recommend the highest honors for our water-purifying equipment. We used a gaso-
line-engined water purification unit which is standard in
the Marine Corps Supply Catalogue. Except for minor,
though of course exasperating, complaints, that spunky
little unit, rigged up by Lieutenant Commander Ed Gleason,
ran for nearly 300 days with a minimum of faltering. The
water was drawn from a rice paddy, passed through a sand-
filter and two chemical feed tanks, and finally through a
chlorination gyzmo before passing into the big 3000-gallon
rubber storage tanks. This was *nouc my* (American water)
which the refugees drank with obvious distaste. They much
preferred the typhoid flavor of the water in certain for-
bidden paddies.

The particular paddy from which our water was lifted
had to be barbed-wired off because the refugees would

wash their feet, food and livestock in it. One morning all the water in that rice paddy was black. We investigated and discovered that the cause was vegetable dye that a peasant had used to color her clothes for the summer Viet Nam fashions. She had dumped the concentrated solution into the rice paddy when she had finished with it. We had to put the camp on water rations until the stuff had cleared.

On several occasions our rubber tanks were slashed, probably maliciously and by pro-Communists. And then again inquisitive kids would climb up the sides of the tanks and drop wooden boats, or occasionally drop themselves, into the water. Great sport! We finally erected a barbed-wire fence around the water tanks.

While we are on the subject of *nouc my*, let me tell you of two of my corpsmen, one of whom was not really a corpsman but an Aviation Boatswain's Mate, Third Class, who was utilized in everything we did. That's Norman M. Baker, at the moment of this writing stationed on the *U.S.S. Philippine Sea.* The other lad was a six-foot-six-inch, two-hundred-pound Swede named Edward Maugre, a hospital corpsman, second class. The refugees loved them. You would see them walking around the camp, probably with sprayers on their backs, surrounded by a mob of shrieking kids. The conventional idea—it's a sound idea—that the children of Viet Nam are irresistible was put in reverse, the children found my corpsmen irresistible.

One day I heard more than the usual uproar of screaming and yelling at the water plant, so I went over to see what was up. Baker and Maugre had decided that the

73

water sediment tanks needed cleaning so they took six of the Vietnamese children, removed their clothes and threw them into the tank, waist deep in water. They handed them brushes and soap and told them to scrub the bottom and side walls. The children were jubilant over the job, and the corpsmen ended by fighting a small war to keep all the other children in the camp from climbing into the tank and joining the soapy six.

Lieutenant Commander Ed Gleason was the sanitation and hygiene expert and at first he was the only man who knew how to solve the occasional maladies of the water-plant equipment. In fact, he constructed the units and nursed them from burping infancy to belching adolescence. When he left, he succeeded in passing on his magic to Baker and Maugre.

The water units were always rather frightening to me. Every time I laid a hand on a lever, either sand would fly out of a hose or the engine would groan and die. So, though I admired the unit from a distance, I left it pretty much to the corpsmen.

When Admiral Sabin visited us on an inspection tour, he asked Maugre what the water tasted like. Maugre replied respectfully, "Dunno, sir, I never touch my own product."

Whenever something went wrong with the unit, I gave Baker my jeep and a carton of cigarettes, and in the voice-of-command I had learned from Dr. Amberson, I'd say: "Baker, get that damned thing fixed—and don't bother me with the details." Hours later, Baker would return with a couple of Legionnaires, all full of cheap brandy and smoking American cigarettes. I never knew where the Frenchmen or the spare parts came from, but the water-machine always became as good as new. And Baker always had an awful hangover which, alas, I am unable to doctor effectively, except in the usual fruitless ways. But he never bothered me with details.

Our first refugee camp became the center of attraction for visiting dignitaries. Admiral Sabin and Commodore Walter Winn, who relieved the Admiral as Commander of the Task Force; General J. Lawton Collins, the former U.S. Army Chief of Staff, who was serving as the President's personal trouble-shooter in Viet Nam, General "Iron Mike" O'Daniel, the Chief of Military Assistance Advisory Group of Saigon, and many other visiting firemen were taken on usually muddy tours of the usually very muddy camp.

The Viet Nam governor of our small area was a patriot by the name of Nguyen Luat. He had been educated in France and chose to return to his own nation of Viet Nam. Before the war, he had been the editor of a newspaper in Hanoi. During the war he had fought with the French as an officer. The Governor came out almost every week and tramped through the camp speaking to his people and lifting their hearts and their spirits.

The Mayor of the city of Haiphong was Mai Van Bot. He would come to the camp often, though without the entourage of the Governor. He was a simple man and a fine one, well loved by the Americans who knew him.

Less well-loved visitors to the camp were Viet Minh

Communist agents. They visited us daily. The refugees would point the first finger of suspicion. They would tell us: "There is a man in Camp de la Pagode Tent 5B who is saying that we have made a great mistake by coming here. He is saying that we should return immediately to fight for the true nationalists, the Viet Minh. He is very strange, this one." The police would find such agents in the camp every couple of days.

The people of Haiphong would come out on their rickshaws and take a look at us to see if living conditions might be better than those in town. I am sure that many moved out to this new housing project.

Vietnamese Public Health, who were desperately short-handed, gave us some native nurses when they could. Like all natives, these girls were so anxious to get to the safety of the south that none of them stayed with us very long. We would find some relatively clean-looking refugees and persuade them to stay on in the camp a month or two, instead of the usual ten days. We would teach them to wash their hands and other basic things; they learned quickly and were always anxious to help. Then we crowned them "nurses." Along with running a camp, being interpreters, father-confessors, American images, doctors, corpsmen, water-plant operators, and the like we thus served as professors of a school of nursing.

After a few weeks the camp was going full force and we were a thriving little community all our own. We had our own name; we had our own government; we had our own hospital, complete with corpsmen and black-toothed, betel-chewing nurses, and we had our own groceries. The daily ration was six hundred grams of rice, meticulously weighed, a couple of fish and such extras as were available.

I have left for the last the most important center in the camp, our church. It was not a great and noble structure— just another tent with its sides rolled up. There was a wooden altar there, and the Blessed Sacrament was reserved by day and night. Every morning, in the shy and early dawn, Mass was said for the camp's fifteen thousand inhabitants. I feel sure God heard the prayers of these poor refugees. They sought no favors. They did not ask God where their children would roam beyond tomorrow's arch, but they thanked Him with strong voices in prayer and in song. They thanked Him for having given them their freedom.

And they turned to the Mother of God, to the Blessed Virgin of Fatima, and said, "Remember, O most gracious Virgin Mary, that never was it known that anyone who fled to Thy protection, implored Thy help, or sought Thy intercession has been left unaided, and we thank Thee, O Queen of Queens."

CHAPTER IX

OUR "TASK FORCE" SHRINKS

With refugees streaming in and others being evacuated, giving the camps a continuing population that ran as high as 15,000, our primary job was to delouse, vaccinate, innoculate them, and screen out those who had communicable diseases. But there was more to it than that. At the sick call tent I was now seeing between 300 and 400 people every day who were desperately in need of medical treatment. What was I to do? Leave them in the camp to die? Send them back behind the Bamboo Curtain?

There is a motto in every service that says (approximately) that a man should keep his mouth shut and his internal system in order and *never* volunteer. Fortunately it is a rule that Americans talk about but seldom observe when things get tough. And I guess I have a special tendency to stick my neck out.

Captain Amberson was worried by my impulsiveness, which was increasing the work-load of the camps. I had argued that the spraying and vaccinating being done in town was haphazard and dangerous; hence no one should be allowed aboard ship without being processed by us. Now I brought the Captain another headache.

"Doctor," I said, "we've got to do something for these sick people. Rules are rules, but we can't surrender a woman and child to the Communists just because the kid has smallpox. We've got to treat the smallpox so that the family can get aboard a ship."

He looked at me wearily, but with obvious understanding. As a doctor he agreed with me heartily. He just felt sorry for a young eager-beaver who thought he could lick every problem in sight.

"All right, Dooley," he said. "Treat the smallpox. You know the limitations as well as I do. Go ahead and do the best you can."

Thus therapy on a vast scale was added to the delousing, vaccination and camp sanitation—at least doubling the dimensions of the medical effort. We stepped up sick call and I enlarged my hospital tent for surgery.

Captain Amberson was suddenly called to Washington, D.C. He was ordered to leave immediately, which meant in twenty-four hours. We scared up a seat on a CAT plane that was taking Chinese Nationals out to Taipeh. Usually I can watch Commanding Officers leave without any emotion whatsoever. When this one left, however, there was the definite feeling of loss—both of an excellent boss, and a good friend. He was replaced by Doctor Britten, who wanted to set up a laboratory for the Fleet Epidemological Disease Control Unit. We couldn't put it out in the camp, because the microscopes and other equipment were very expensive and there was too much chance of theft.

The French Navy Base was the solution. Admiral Querville was most cooperative and gave us an empty warehouse. Here we established our portable lab and brought the specimens that we collected in the camps to be analyzed and catalogued.

The laboratory didn't look much like Bethesda Naval Medical Center but it was functional. We had large wooden tables, several hard folding chairs. For the boss, we stole a large velvet-covered couch which looked as if it had come from Emperor Gia Long's throne room.

Commander Sidney Britten, Dr. Amberson's successor, was a lab man from way back; his main interest was in the epidemological end of the work, just as Captain Amberson's main interest was in field work, such as teaching JG's how to build refugee tent camps. Doctor Britten took over the lab at the Navy base and left sick-call and the running of the camp pretty much to me.

I spent most of the day holding sick call, except for a couple of hours during the heat of the afternoon. It was during this breathing spell that the mandarin who was Chief of the Camp gave me my Vietnamese lessons. He spoke impeccable French and this was our common denominator. With some concerted effort over a couple of months, I was able to speak Vietnamese as well as I needed to, with an adequate Tonkin accent. It is a very easy, monosyllabic language. I even learned some Vietnamese songs.

At this time our days had a persisting and often amusing pattern. Dr. Britten would head a group who would drive out to the camp with determined jaws set. He would sit in the sick-call tent, in the 105 degrees of humid heat, wearing a jungle cap, green Marine fatigues, and with boots and trousers tucked in the tops in an attempt to escape being eaten alive by the malarial mosquitoes, which were about as large and deadly as small jet fighters.

He would direct his corpsmen, James Cobb, of Los Angeles, Joseph Milo, of Lynn, Massachusetts, Donald Whitlock, of La Sunta, California, Walt Hoban of Philadelphia, Art Prichett and Robert Prusso—I am not sure where they hailed from—while they collected venous and peripheral blood smears. They would use these for studies and send hundreds of the answers back to fill the shopping lists of National Naval Medical School. I understand that this work resulted in at least two medical discoveries, one of considerable importance.

Meanwhile I would stand out in the camp and, with candy, try to entice the children to give us stool specimens. In this sometimes ludicrous job I was assisted by my corpsman, Dennis D. Shepard, a Salem, Oregon, boy, and a very fine one too.

My Vietnamese was then pretty poor. I knew how to say "stool" and "sample" and "give me" and, of course, "please." But when I combined these words into a sentence, I would evoke howls of laughter. I would just have to repeat the words, point and grunt, and then go through the process all over again. Shepard would nod, point, smile and pass out candy and small paper boxes. Some of the children would take these containers, given for another purpose, and put the candy into them. Others would take aim and spit into them. "No, no," I would say. "Stool specimens."

Then some would disappear with the boxes and return them with either microscopic or overflowing contents. But most of the refugees would just disappear, boxes and all. I am afraid that Dr. Britten was disappointed with my end of the collection operation.

Lieutenant Richard Kaufman, of Pittsburgh, also of the Medical Service Corps, was in Dr. Britten's unit. He and Lt. Comdr. Gleason spent a good deal of time crawling along the pipes of the city's inadequate water and sewage systems. Dick also placed rat traps all over the place, even in the hotel we lived in. He would catch the pony-sized rats alive, then comb their luxurious coats for fleas which might indicate the presence of plague.

Chief Cobb and Hospital Corpsman First Class Joe Milo were deeply interested in mosquitoes, both in the malaria-bearing kind and in those that carried yellow fever. They set up mosquito traps around the latrines, the water plant, the sick-call tent, our hotel rooms and other choice spots.

Don Whitlock, Hospitalman Second Class, spent hours peering into his microscope at blood smears, cataloguing percentages and so on.

So we were a strange lot, we Americans; Shepard and I armed with our stool specimen cups, Cobb and Milo with their bottles of mosquitoes, Whitlock with his slides, Dr. Britten with vials of blood, Ed Gleason with maps of the city's sewers, Dick Kaufman with his live rats. At this moment there is probably some refugee in Saigon writing a book about his experiences with those amazing inhabitants of the United States who came to Haiphong with their incredible customs and even more incredible collection mania.

By the end of October we had collected thousands of specimens of every nature and kind—fully enough, Doctor Britten decided. At this time the French Navy informed Admiral Sabin that the situation with the Communists in this still-free zone was getting very sticky, and that it might be better if there were fewer Americans in Haiphong, though we only numbered about twenty all told. The French, and we too for that matter, lived in a vague but constant dread that the Viet Minh would "liberate" this port any day and take us captive. The Viet Minh had already taken over the Tonkin's capital, Hanoi, less than an hour away, shrinking the free zone to just a few miles around Haiphong. General René Cogny called Haiphong into a state of "guarded emergency."

Ed Gleason left a few weeks after Dr. Amberson flew to Washington. Commander Britten and Lieutenant Kaufman returned to Japan in October and took with them all of the corpsmen who were part of the FEDCU unit.

I was left with only three corpsmen to help me—Dennis Shepard, a new arrival, Peter Kessey, who was superb, and noble Norman Baker who was to be with me to the bitter end. Now a Naval medical officer of one year's vintage was in sole command of the refugee camp and related functions. He was subject to the directives of superiors, but in practice he was left almost wholly to his own devices. By guess and by God, I kept the unit running for the remaining eight months.

Daily I expected new brass to arrive and take over, but no one came. Much later I heard from Admiral Sabin himself what had happened. Captain Amberson had told him: "The situation in Haiphong is extremely dangerous and the fewer men we have ashore the better. Young Dooley has the situation well in hand and can carry on."

Sure enough, in mid-November orders came through designating me "Commander, Task Unit 90. 8. 6." The decimal points indicated I was far down the line, but I was pretty proud. Then some lunkhead, undoubtedly a line Lieut. Commander, decided that for security reasons our mission would be known as Operation Cockroach. Damn!

CHAPTER X

THE POWER OF PROPAGANDA

Often in the early evening when the day's work was done, I would go to the tents with the mandarin Chief of the Camp and talk to the people who had just arrived from the Communist zone. The refugees, really escapees, were just as interested in me as I was in them. I asked them what their life had been like under the Viet Minh rule.

Thus I was able to learn a good deal about the people of the Tonkin, who had come under the heel of Communist oppression. I was able to understand the confusion in their minds and in their nation. They scarcely knew friends from enemies. Natural pride in their own country had been exploited until it became hate for any other nation, especially for France and for the United States, since the U.S. supplied the French with tanks and guns and planes used in the colonial war.

Perhaps some of these natives had helped to bring the new Communist police state into being, but their hope and faith had turned to suspicion and disillusionment. To them,

Ho Chi Minh and his forces had represented nationalism. The "Benevolent Aid" that the Viet Minh had accepted from Red China had seemed benevolent indeed. Hadn't China accepted similar aid from Russia and hadn't this helped to create the new and glorious Red China? At least, the Viet Minh radio always said that Red China was glorious.

The Communists knew just how to handle the average Tonkinese rice-delta family. They played upon the pride of such families in their fields. They promised agrarian reforms. They promised to divide lands belonging to the colonial rich among the native poor. And this was done. However, the poor were soon burdened with such a tax that their pocket money at the end of the harvest was less than it had been before.

The Viet Minh promised the water wheel. This was to be a great thing for the land. The Tonkin is divided into small paddies, each about the size of a football field. Small mud dikes around the fields separate one from another. During the life of a rice crop, there are times when it must be in water and times when it must be dry. So at various times the water must be transferred from one field to another. If the receiving field is lower than the other, there is not much difficulty. But if it is level or higher, the water must be transferred by hand, with buckets. The transfer goes on for hours at a time, and it has been going on for centuries.

Ho Chi Minh said: "I will give you a water wheel. This will ease your labors. It will lift the water for you." And when he took over he did give water wheels to thousands

The determination of the men of Viet Nam: determined to worship their God, determined to be free, determined to escape to be so.

By sampans down the myriad fingers of the Red River; through jungle roads, across rice fields, the exodus took place. . . .

They have escaped on rafts, hurriedly made by lashing together
bamboo poles.

Here is a transfer, four miles out to sea. Over 15,000 have sailed from the coast of Bui Chu.

They reached the eerie, fairyland-like Baie d'Along, four hours down river from Haiphong, the portal to their freedom.

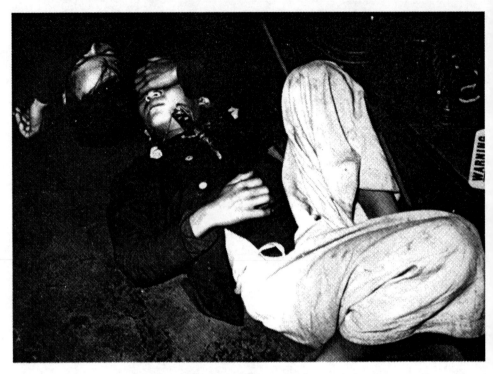

Fatigue after escape . . . with the ever-present symbol of Jesus Christ.

When they arrived in Haiphong they came to my huge camps, deep in the monsoon mud.

The row of medical tents, my "hospital," with the ever-present drainage ditches. Processing took place, then transfer to U. S. ships.

Flooding of the camp was our constant plague. Epidemics were imminent. Yet none occurred during our year there.

It was never hard to find water to bathe a child in. The monsoons furnished enough. Norman Baker's chlorinated-water-plant made more.

Two of my best nurses. Called nurses because they knew how to wash and did so, weekly.

The faces of the women of the Tonkin, whose men have been slaughtered in the eight years of war.

A grandmother of North Viet Nam. The same as grandmothers everywhere. Yet here is wretchedness.

This lad is not sure about anything just yet, especially that canned American milk.

Although most believed in us finally, there were always the incredulous, the dangerous.

Every refugee carried some heraldry of their belief in God. This belief gave them strength to escape.

Cooking à la style of North Viet Nam. Birds' eyes, bats' wings, Bun Tang vermicelli soup . . . fish heads.

This face asks "Can I believe in the Americans, can I trust
them? Whom shall I trust . . .?"

The shuttle service . . . small French craft for the four-hour
trip from Haiphong to the anchorage of the American ship.

Desolation and apprehension . . . this is infancy in the Red-devoured Tonkin.

Rice, enough for all . . . American aid. Hungry hands, starvation-swollen bellies . . . the children of Viet Nam.

This man had been so badly beaten he could not walk. Refusing to be carried, he crawled out with shoes on his hands.

My "hard corps of agents." Out to a U. S. ship for a party, then back to the camps to spread the word of the love of the American sailor.

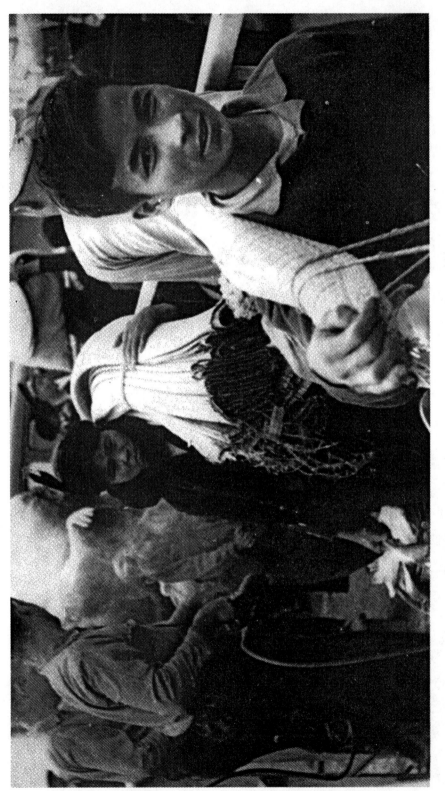

Dusting with DDT. "Will it make us sterile, as the Viet Minh said it would?"

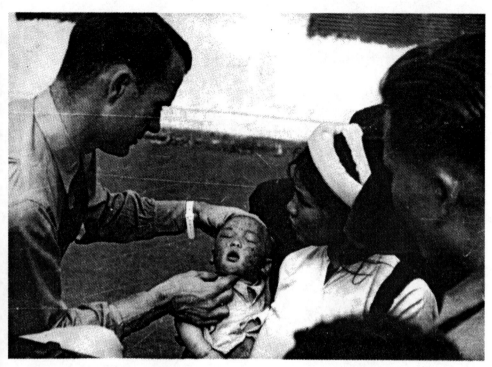

Skin infections kept my sick-call lengthy, and sad. So much still needed to be done.

Bone infection, from an inadequately treated two-year-old infection.

Miracle penicillin, a gift from Pfizer, whom the Viet Minh
called "a capitalistic American monster company."

Smallpox, constantly present, but never in epidemic proportions.

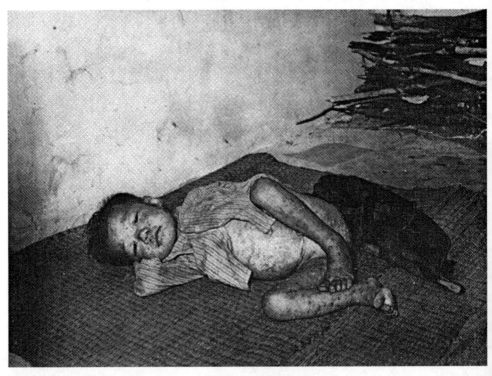

Lia with her new "American leg" on the transport. Who looks happier, Lia or the sailors?

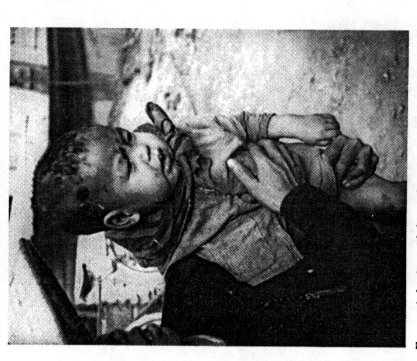

Fungus infections of the scalp, present in the majority of children. Soap is one of the cures.

Christmas Day, 1954, the only day I put on a blouse and pressed my pants. Reason? A party for me at the orphanage.

Erma Koyna's gift of clothes arriving at the orphanage of
Madame Ngai. Such opulence.

Two more tykes arriving; parents' whereabouts unknown . . .
Two more orphans for Ngai. "He ain't heavy, he's m'brother."

Finally on the U. S. transports, the refugees look through a hawse-hole at the uncertain future.

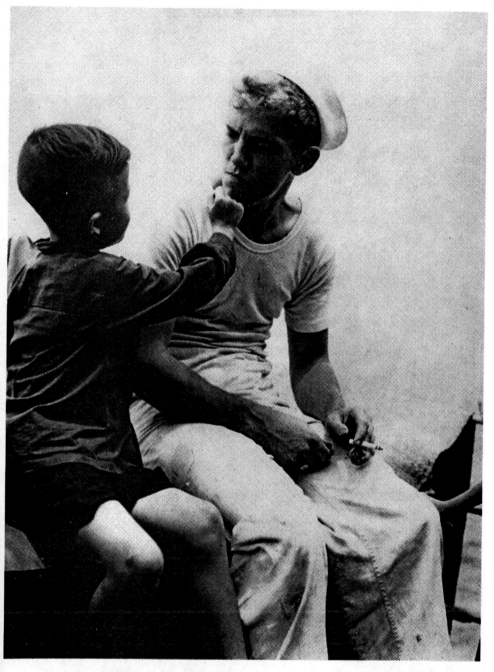

This child had been told that American sailors would roast him alive. Now he doesn't believe it. But he did.

Blinded by trachoma, this fellow eats American rice . . . and with a spoon.

Madame Ngai's orphans entertaining American sailors. Madame Ngai and her benefactor (who wasn't?) Lt. Ted Torok are in the background.

This poor sailor made the mistake of growing a beard—an object of fascination to the kids.

Norman Baker, a fine sailor, a good American, my constant companion. my helping hand, and my friend.

Saigon, May, 1955: President Ngo Dinh Diem awarding me his nation's highest award, "Officier de l'Ordre National de Viet Nam." It is I who am grateful.

of farmers. There was one metaphorical flaw in them. As they belonged to the state, it was only simple justice for the state to ask the farmer, as his end of the bargain, to pay the state a certain percentage of his crops. As can well be imagined, that percentage was not small.

And so, as more and more of the promised "reforms" were put into effect, more and more of the Tonkinese began to dream of escape. The so-called guarantee of free and unmolested passage was now clearly a farce and ours were probably the only camps in history that people had to escape *into*.

Meanwhile, the Communists bombarded the people with stories of the imperialistic French and Americans who were kidnapping Tonkinese citizens. They hammered the stories home, hour after hour, month after month. All young men and women were required to attend "re-education" classes every morning. Here the political commissars reiterated again and again their stories about the American barbarians.

To rice-paddy peasants, some of the stories sounded pretty plausible. Americans are known to be obsessed with the subject of cleanliness, so perhaps they do cut the hands from those who vomit on their ships. America is a land of tremendous manufacturing operations, so perhaps Americans do need coolies for slave labor. It fits the picture—the boot fits the foot.

Their propaganda campaign was next to agrarian reform in importance. To be efficacious propaganda must be one-sided. Those exposed to its fiery tongue must never be allowed to hear any other tongue. The curtain which crashed down on Asia had the same impact, though of bamboo, as the Iron Curtain had in Europe.

One thing did pierce this curtain. The refugees told me of secret battery radios, smuggled in to them just lately, on which they would listen to the Voice of America. By this means they learned of the evacuation, and of the promises of Geneva. When they arrived at our camps they eyed us cautiously, and sometimes with active dislike. They were probably thinking, "Look at that sailor the young Doctor calls Baker. See him going around with that spraying—maybe disease-spraying—machine on his back. What deviltry is he capable of?"

He wasn't capable of much. Norman Baker, Aviation Boatswain's Mate, Third Class, is first-class in my book, or maybe first-class plus. He was sent to me early in the game as, of all things, my French interpreter. The person who sent him must have been the only one in the line of command who did not realize that my facility in French was the main reason I was here in the first place.

Baker and I decided it was the obligation of neither of us to set matters straight. "All right, so I won't interpret," he said in substance, "but I think I might be useful in other ways." It was the understatement of the year. Baker is the American sailor who was the real hero of Haiphong.

All my corpsmen felt the people's unrest and fear. We might be holding sick-call and see an old woman, perhaps a leper, squatting on her haunches watching us closely. She might stay for hours, watching us clean, inject, treat and

dress the refugees. After some time and with much hesi-
tancy, she might come up and ask for something for her
"dao mat," or trachomatous eyes. Even then, she was full
of doubt.

However, the "miraculousness" of our drugs was a great
persuader. I had never thought much about the power of
antibiotics, vitamins, soap, cleanliness and the rest of it.
They have power unbridled.

Vaccination afforded a special problem, as the people
had been told that we would inject diseases into them if
they came into our camps. American bacteriological warfare! We were reported to be carrying out large-scale
medical experiments and using the Tonkinese as guinea
pigs. That was also one reason why it was so hard to collect
specimens for FEDCU. Specimens, for Heaven's sake, for
what?

They were so wary of us that it was often difficult to get
them into the sick-call tent for treatment. So we would hold
sick-call in *front* of the tent. Then some ten thousand
refugees could squat on their haunches all around us and
observe "What will he do?" "Watch him . . ." "Be careful . . ."

As for those stories about ships with huge mouths that
spewed people overboard—well, no wonder that, when the
refugees first sighted the LCTs and LSMs opening their
bow doors to embark them, they would surge back in a
wave of fear.

A priest would stand on a truck with a loudspeaker and
talk and talk, sometimes for hours, during embarkations,

telling the people to go aboard and not to be afraid. He would often get down and walk aboard for a moment himself in order to set an example. So the refugees would go aboard too, but fearfully, every step of the way.

Often they had leaflets that they had been issued behind the Curtain. The leaflets were downright absurd, but still...

One showed the American ship *Marine Adder*, a transport. It showed violently seasick refugees leaning over the rail vomiting. They had their hands braced on the rail. Sailors with white hats, the devils, were cutting the hands off the people as they braced themselves on the rail. Things are tough all over.

Even the refugees who did not literally believe this nonsense were never quite sure. Some of the younger ones, who might loosely be termed intellectuals, would quiz me about the atomic bomb. They had heard that the Atomic Control Commission had completely destroyed the State of Nevada. Then it had annihilated Bikini and other islands in the Pacific. Was it true that the next explosion was to be in the Tonkin? They just wondered. "Why did they ask?" They held up a leaflet. A piece of Viet Minh propaganda showing an aerial view of their ancient, and beloved capital of Hanoi. Over it were the three concentric circles of Atomic destruction. Printed on this was just one word that all could read—"My" which means "American."

They even felt suspicious about the simple white Navy skivvy undershirt. I gave a talk downriver on the *U.S.S. Askari*, a repair ship. Partially to thank me, but mostly because of a sailor's eager willingness to help, the crew

122

of the ship sent me a coffin-sized locker box stuffed with Navy cotton T-shirts and underpants.

The refugees certainly needed them, the shirts at least and, if not so badly, the shorts also. The box reached the camp and the refugees gathered around. I handed one of them an undershirt. He took it in his hands and looked at it, mute. He didn't feel the material. He didn't hold it up like an American woman in a department store buying a bra. He just held it in his hands and watched me closely.

Sensing disaster, I tried something. I took my own khaki shirt off in front of the mob and showed them that I was wearing a white T shirt with my name and service number stenciled across the front. It was just like the ones I was passing out. I said a little prayer, hoping that this would do it, and maybe the prayer did. A boy held his shirt up and another slipped one over his bare torso. Soon the shirts were going like nylons in a bargain sale. Thank God it worked—I had no intentions of showing them my skivvies.

I wish the boys on the *Askari* could have seen the kids, customarily bare bottomed, running around the camp in Navy shorts (usually on backwards, for the sake of efficiency) and the girls in T-shirts with "Sam Goldblatz, BM3, 278-00-19," or "Jack Flanagan, FN, 339-27-61," stenciled across their bosoms.

Mike Adler's successor, Roger Ackley, arrived from Germany, where he had been dealing with refugee problems. He was a large and jovial man. Much of the joviality left him after he had taken a hard professional look at the abject misery around us. He coined the expression "American Impact." We four of the medical unit, the first Americans most of the refugees had ever seen, were in an excellent position to contribute to the American Impact. My boys and I sat down and figured out a plan. I suppose an Admiral of the Line would say, "We promulgated a feasible policy." The boys were quick to see that every move they made was considered a move by America, that their every action had massive reactions. If they pushed the children roughly away, or splashed women with a jeep's wheels, or blasted its horn at them when they squatted in the road, that was America pushing, splashing, blasting; it would reflect on our nation as a whole. It was hard to be patient with the throngs that followed us everywhere we went, even to the bathroom (that field over there to the left of the camp). Yet I never saw a man lose his temper.

My boys treated the refugees with patience, understanding and a little love. This was a largely negative approach. We had a positive approach as well. We began our own little program of selling America. It began with the expression, in Vietnamese, "This is American Aid." All my boys learned the expression and repeated it every time they did anything from passing out an APC to helping a child pull his pants back up when they fell down. In fact, we used it so often that when the refugees, in turn, would give us a bowl of rice, or help put up a new tent, or push my jeep out of the monsoon mud, they would grin and roar, "This is Vietnamese Aid."

Roger Ackley obtained many small American Aid emblems. They were nailed to boxes, plastered on bottles of

124

medicines, attached to the water tent, fount of that cursed *nouc my*.

You couldn't really say that we were staffed and organized like the Pentagon for a really big educational effort, but I believe our sliver of salesmanship was of prime importance. Rival ideologies are fighting this war now and *not* with guns and hydrogen bombs either. They are competing for the souls of those who are rising in search of a better life. So we have to demonstrate that *our* way of life has qualities that are good.

This the men of the Preventive Medicine Unit understood. And this, to the best of their abilities, they did. I salute them for it.

On a radio broadcast from Hanoi, now the Communist capital, there was a nightly program called Voice of Viet Nam. I remember one broadcast. It was on a so-called "Art and Literary Program," for the rice peasants of the delta. The subject was, "This is an American." I quote its text word for word:

"His head is a blockhouse. His beard is barbed wire. His eyes are bombs. His teeth are dum-dum bullets. His two arms are guns and from his nose flames shoot out. A vampire, he sucks the blood of little children. His forehead is a nest of artillery and his body is an airfield. His fingers are bayonets, his feet tanks. He puts his fangs out in order to threaten, but in his hideous mouth he can only chew scrap iron because he has against him the powerful forces of our people of Viet Nam, who are valiantly fighting. All things considered, the American is a paper giant."

125

Hey you, out there in Tucson, Kenosha and Des Moines! Do you recognize yourself from this description? Eaten any good babies lately?

Well, the refugees had no radios, so they didn't hear that particular broadcast. I don't believe they would have given much credence to it anyway. Baker's head didn't look like a blockhouse. He is, and looks like, a kindly sort of guy. My nose gives forth no flames. And most of the rest of the medical unit gave up sucking the blood of little children as soon as the Republicans were elected.

The Viet Minh propaganda even began to affect the International Control Committee of Canadians, Poles and Indians, set up by the Geneva treaty. The committeemen visited our camp frequently to investigate Communist claims that we were doing this or that to the detriment of the refugees. They investigated a claim that we were polluting the water with poison (that one left Ed Maugre speechless). They investigated a claim that we were spraying the refugees with a powder that rendered them sterile. We were spraying them with a powder all right—DDT—and perhaps it rendered their body lice a bit sterile.

And then there was that old standby—the Americans and French were forcing the refugees to leave the Tonkin. We were kidnapping them. Here is a quotation from the Viet Nam News Agency broadcast of November 27, 1954:

"The French Union forces and the agents of the U.S. imperialists have been endeavoring to carry out raids and kidnappings in the Haiphong perimeter, forcing the population to evacuate to South Vietnam. At 9 p.m. last night

126

they mobilized armed police and police agents to encircle Du Hang Street and took away 50 youths. They shamelessly declared that 'the youths must enroll in the army, otherwise they will be drafted to work in the rubber plantations in South Vietnam.'

"In five days, the imperialists' agents arrested 117 pedicab drivers and brought them to the south. According to still incomplete figures, 551 persons in Haiphong have been caught in 21 raids in one month.

"In Kien An three raids were carried out during the same periods, and 99 persons were arrested, while in Quang Yen others were victims of similar measures.

"The Vietnamese people of the Haiphong perimeter, as well as those throughout the country, strongly protest against these Fascist activities and urge the French Union forces immediately to cease their raids, kidnappings and forcible evacuations that seriously encroach upon the Geneva armistice agreement."

We had many raids and riots in Haiphong, but I don't have to tell you that we never forcefully evacuated anyone. On the contrary; believe me, on the contrary. Many a night, after I had done a fourteen- or fifteen-hour trick in sick-call, I would have been overjoyed to see the evacuation come to an instant stop. I was fed up. If I was an imperialist—how, outside expanding Russia, do you go about being an imperialist nowadays?—I never felt much like one. I felt like a dog-tired, half-baked, rather frightened young doctor.

But the truth, I guess, strange as it sounds even to myself,

127

is that I was enjoying the burden, and more so as it waxed heavier. I enjoyed it in the sense that a cross-channel swimmer enjoys his swim even when his breath labors and his limbs are numb. My growing fear was that a newcomer, no matter how able, might not feel as strongly as I did about the fugitives and the things they were fleeing. What, I asked myself, if he could not see through the rags and sores and stench to the soul of Viet Nam, as I was beginning to glimpse it? The sort of outer force that my Navy orders represented was replaced by my own inner compulsion to finish the job.

Again and again I went to French or the two American officials to complain about something, only to emerge with one more responsibility on my agenda. For example, I thought at one point that the handling of rice was inefficient and unfair. "Give me the job and I'll see to it myself," I said in a flareup. I was taken at my hasty word and thereafter managed the rice rations.

But it is true, as I say, that we did have riots, or near-riots, at Haiphong. The first time we set up the compressed air motors and the DDT dusting machines we had a near-riot on our hands. Ed Gleason was the boss of this operation and he had a dusting-gun in hand to lead his corpsmen, who were lined up behind him with six more. The idea was that as the refugees passed down a line they would be given a good going-over with DDT to help keep down louse-born epidemics.

In the first group of refugees were several small children. When they got alongside Ed he pushed the trigger on

128

his gun and swirls of white dust flew down on the kids. Their mother had a long balance pole across her shoulder with a basket hanging on each end. When she saw this American blowing powder on her children (she had heard of that particular American atrocity), she took off after Ed, swinging that pole like everything.

I laughed so hard that I lost track of exactly what happened then. I think that after a blow or two Ed managed to get his arms around her, polka fashion, and the chief mandarin and his men helped to break up the fight. Then Ed dusted his corpsmen thoroughly to demonstrate the benign nature of this powder to human beings. The corpsmen didn't dust Ed.

Baker and I also took some beatings, not all of them minor, at the hands of these misguided and hysterical people. But, remembering the importance of "face" in the Orient, we were always careful to take up where we left off.

One day a woman brought me a baby whose body was covered with ulcers. Yaws and ulcers respond miraculously to penicillin and this looked like a routine case. I gave the infant a shot in the buttocks and told the mother to bring it back the next day.

A few hours later, l heard shouts and curses, and saw the woman holding the baby aloft for the people to see. Here was proof that I was an American monster! The child had reacted to the penicillin with an angry-looking, though quite harmless, case of hives. The distraught mother was in no mood for explanations. She handed her baby to a bystander, grabbed a stout stick and called up a dozen sympathizers. When Baker rescued me at last, I had broken ribs, black eyes and miscellaneous bruises.

The next day, with the whole camp watching, I went to the woman's tent alone and unarmed. As I expected, the hives had disappeared and the horrible ulcers were healing nicely. The woman burst into tears, and fell at my feet begging forgiveness. She remained in the camp for weeks, serving as one of my helpers at sick-call, always eager to exhibit her nice clean baby. The effect on the refugees was worth the fractured ribs.

CHAPTER XI

THE STORY OF CUA LO VILLAGE

The French Navy was constantly on the alert for escapees in the waters along the free enclave. They had patrol craft and a seaplane conducting a continuing search for sampans which looked as if they were seeking haven.

In the early months, the refugees floated down the river's many tributaries into Haiphong, but as the Viet Minh controls tightened this became impossible. So the braver people set sail from their coasts in sampans not built for the bold winds of the South China Seas.

Captain Gerald Cauvin of the French Navy was in charge of this particular operation and he kept us informed of his activities. This was a great help to me at the camp because it warned me what to expect.

Early one morning, Cauvin sent a man to our camp to take me to the French Navy pier. He said he had just received a radio message that there were fourteen large junks out in the Baie d'Along.

Cauvin was sending down a French craft, an LSM, to meet

131

the junks and bring them to Haiphong. I alerted the camp
to expect five hundred or so very sick people (actually
there were more than eleven hundred). Then Captain
Cauvin and I went aboard the LSM and sailed four hours
down the river to the bay. The seaplane that had spotted
the refugees meanwhile had returned to Haiphong.

We arrived in the bay about noon. It was absolutely
silent, this strange place with its bare rocks jutting high—
no foliage, no vegetation, just barren grey stones. They
were like giant stalagmites piercing the water's surface,
needling toward the sky.

The sampans had sailed into the bay, one behind the
other. They were huddled together. Several of the boats
were lashed end to end. As we headed toward them, we
observed them closely through our binoculars. The brilliant noonday sun on the clear water made this a storybook
fairyland, but what we saw was hardly a storybook sight.

Jammed onto these fourteen sampans were more than
a thousand refugees who had sailed an unbelievable two
hundred miles in the turbulent South China Seas. They did
this in these small fishing junks, risking all dangers, against
all odds, accomplishing the near-impossible. Though they
were in the warm sun, they were drenched and cold. The
sea had made them so deathly sick that they had vomited
their stomachs dry. Even from a distance, you could see
that the coldness of the night had made them stiffen in
every joint and ache in every bone. They moved around
the sampans helping one another, yet in the mass they
seemed immobile, sprawled over the wooden decks.

132

It was as if they moved in a slow-motion picture. The constant soaking in salt water during all hours of day and night had made their skins dry, and the blazing sun of noon had cracked it. The continuous immersion of their feet made their ankles swell and bloat. We could feel the misery of their situation even before we touched them.

When our LSM was close enough for the refugees to make out the French flag on our stern, a heart-warming thing happened. Recognizing us as friends and not as foes, they hoisted, on a broken spar their own drenched flag; a flag they had hidden for years . . . their symbol, their emblem, their heraldry.

To the top of their highest mast they hauled the Papal banner, a yellow and gold flag displaying the Pope's tiara and the keys of Saint Peter.

As we pulled alongside, eager French hands reached down to help these people into the well-deck of the LSM. Most of the refugees were transferred to our ship. Some of the healthier men were left aboard a few of the sampans, which were lashed to the sides of the LSM. We headed back to Haiphong with our load.

We handed out tea, water and French rolls to the escapees. Though they were inadequate in amount, they helped. The little LSM with a crew of only two dozen did not carry large food stocks. How I wished I had thought to bring along a hundred sacks of rice.

Cauvin and I found several elders who seemed to be the leaders. These we took to the cabin and asked: "Where did

133

you sail from? What was life like in your village? Why
have you come? Who are you?"

They told us their story, in sad and weary voices, as
though they had repeated it a thousand times. In a slow
monotone, in good French, they told us about their lives.
We listened for three hours.

The story was not especially new; we had heard similar
stories from other escapees. But there was a poignancy here
that was even greater than usual. Their escape was planned
and executed entirely without outside aid; with only two
ancient tools, faith and hope.

Though at this moment I am thousands of miles and
thousands of hours away, I can vividly remember nearly
every word. The old men with wrinkled, haggard faces sat
across from us, sipping their strong tea, speaking softly,
unhesitatingly:

"Cua Lo is our village. It is about 300 kilometers south
of here, on the sea coast. It was a happy village years ago.
Our landscape is flat, divided into an infinite number of
small rice paddies, often brilliant green with the rice crops.
Overhead, during the dark grey season of the monsoon,
damp clouds scud across the sky. During the hot season the
sun shines forth in all her splendor and our skies are clear
blue. All day you can see our people working in the fields,
irrigating their crops and plowing in the red-brown mud
behind squelching water buffaloes.

"Others in our village were fishermen. These junks we
have come on belong to them. The junks are strong, have
two masts and large mustard-colored sails. But they are

134

crudely built, and are not meant for the high waters of an open sea.

"Our enemies became our rulers in 1951. They gave us a new set of laws, a new history, a new way of life . . . the Communist way of life. Yet the Communists say it is Viet Minh Nationalism. This was a dull uncertain peace. It is all very confusing, even for us, the mandarins, who are supposed to be intelligent.

"Now anything at all that had been concerned with the French became tainted. In the eyes of our new historians, everything the whites had done was evil. Even the good they had done was evil, for it had been done only out of sordid self-interest.

"True the French introduced some medical science to Viet Nam, and conducted campaigns against epidemics. But this, we were told, was done only so that they could obtain sound coolies and healthy slaves.

"Our new way of life was supposed to be Utopia. But it did not take long to see that the underlying idea was that the present generation must always be pitilessly sacrificed to the happiness of the one that is to come.

"The new land reforms produced only famine, which now claws at the belly of all our people. Their 'materialism' became an ogre which sucked our land dry. At first the attainments of Viet Minh nationalism seemed to conform to authentic justice. Then it would show itself in true form—a lie. The new sociology has led to family denunciations, self-criticism and distrust. The people of our village have been ruthlessly sacrificed to the idea of economic

135

utility. Never before has there been cruelty of this organized order.

"We all had one thought—to escape—and so for weeks we made preparations. Every day we hid away small balls of rice. There could be no open talk of escape; nothing could be done straightforwardly. All had to be done by stealth, since the village was run by a mandarin who, though he was an old friend of ours, was now a Viet Minh commissar, and had been made cruel and warped by his new beliefs. Everywhere he had agents stationed, in the market place, in nearly every hut.

"We made plans but could not hold meetings. According to the new laws, there could be no gatherings of more than four people. We passed the word while we bent our backs in the rice fields, or while our fishermen unloaded their catch, or while our women visited in the market place.

"Finally plans and prayers reached a climax. The night had come. There was no moon, the sky was dark and the seas were calm. From eleven o'clock until one the next morning, we slipped down to our boats singly or in twos. Meanwhile a lad named Mai Van Thinh, loudly singing and shouting, was creating a disturbance at one end of the village. This drew the police, the Commissar and many soldiers to see what was going on. Meanwhile our boats loaded.

"These junks were built to handle about twenty-five people each. That night they each carried more than a hundred. As quiet as the night itself, we slipped away from the shore and headed out into the South China Sea.

"Yes, we escaped from the village successfully. How-ever, we were not especially jubilant, because our thoughts were with Mai. Sooner or later his part in our escape would become known. Then what would be his fate?

"Mai's father and mother had been killed in the war, and in 1953 his only brother, Cham, had been burned alive, apparently because he was the head of a Christian youth movement. On the afternoon of January 16, 1953, he was tied to a tree and brutally beaten with short bamboo sticks. Then his blood-soaked body was splashed with gasoline, ignited, and he was burned to death.

"Using both oars and sails, as rapidly as we could we headed straight out to the open sea, eager to get beyond the three-mile limit to international waters. By morning we could not see land and we felt comparatively safe. That is, we were safe from one danger; we had the sea to struggle with now.

"We wanted to sail north and we had had no compass or nor any extensive knowledge of navigation. However, we turned to put the sun at our right hand and headed for Haiphong, where we knew the French and Americans would be willing to help. They would take us all the way to Saigon.

"Our trip lasted five days and five long nights. We could not have fires, for our wood was too wet. We were forced to eat our rice when it was damp and soggy. Our tea was soaked with salt and only served to increase our illness. We had little drinking water or none. The decks of our small junks were splashed by every wave. We were miserable.

137

"Early this morning we found ourselves in this strange place and knew we must have reached the legendary Baie d'Along. When we saw your seaplane we were sure. And now we are free. . . ."

Quietly the mandarins told us this story. With awe we listened to this recital of magnificent courage and hope.

And now a chant came from the well-deck of the LSM, a soft hymn that the mass of refugees were singing. We all walked out on deck and listened. I could not make out all the Vietnamese words. The mandarins hummed with the song and then translated it into French for us.

The people were offering their thanks to God for His help during this crisis in their lives. They chanted: "Oh, Lord, we love the beauty of Thy house and the place where Thy glory dwells. Provide that our days be spent in peace with Thee."

CHAPTER XII

PHAT DIEM'S LONGEST
HOLY DAY

In Haiphong, the port city of Viet Nam's Tonkin delta, the languages to be heard seemed as varied as those on the Tower of Babel. French forces were still present, though not in great numbers. We Americans, although just a handful, managed to make our own voices heard above most of the others. The priests who ran the Catholic Mission—Father Felice, Father Lopez and their assistants—were from the Philippines and spoke Spanish.

Then there were the three-man teams of the International Control Commission, which contained representatives of one democratic country, Canada; one Communist country, Poland; and one supposedly neutral country, India. One day, in a group of twenty people, I heard the following languages spoken: English, French, Vietnamese, Indian, Polish, Sikh and German. No Spanish that morning—Father Felice wasn't there.

The International Control Commission was set up by the

signatories of the Geneva treaty in July of 1954. Its long
title was usually abbreviated to "CIC." It was to be the
responsibility of this commission to enter all the areas of
Indo-China during the next two years and report back to
Geneva. The Commission was to make observations in both
parts of tragically divided Viet Nam, and also to conduct
investigations into the countries of Laos and Cambodia.
It had no police power or military power but, in theory
at least, it had a great deal of diplomatic prestige.

The Commission kept fixed teams of observers in Saigon,
Hanoi, the capitals of Cambodia and Laos and other large
cities. Then it had mobile teams which would travel from
one spot to another on both sides of the parallel to satisfy
themselves that the terms of the Geneva treaty were being
faithfully carried out. The election planned for Viet Nam
in 1956 was to be supervised by the CIC. According to the
plan, in casting over 22 million votes the people of North
and South Viet Nam would decide whether their country
would unite or remain divided. They would also choose the
kind of regime under which they wanted to live. There was
not the shadow of a doubt that the 10 million in the Communist north would "decide" in favor of a continuation of
the Communist regime—the Communist bosses would see
to that. What would be decided in the south was another
story.

In theory, anyone who wanted to see members of the
Commission's teams had the right to do so at any time. So
anyone who might have a complaint against either side

would be able to air this complaint in the presence of international representatives.

Like so much in Indo-China, this looked extremely good on paper. In practice it left something to be desired. The Commission was highly effective in some ways, but in the field of helping the refugees who wanted to move south, it was inadequate.

The Viet Minh had a healthy respect for the Commission and its teams, since they had the power of appealing to world opinion. If the world is aware that, despite their promises, the Communists did *not* freely release Tonkinese for the refugee evacuation, the Commission must get credit for the fact. In enlightening world opinion, the Commission has done a superb job. Those of us in Haiphong knew at first hand that it was telling the truth because the refugees who escaped would describe their experiences to us and we had to treat many of those who did attempt to escape and were caught and punished.

But all the CIC could do was to find out the facts and report them. It had no power to force the Viet Minh to allow the refugees to leave.

If CIC representatives were visiting a certain village, they might set up a council table in the public square and spread the word that anyone who wished to talk to them could come and do so. But just outside the square the Viet Minh might erect road-blocks to keep out villagers and people from nearby cantons. The Viet Minh would claim that the road-blocks were for the protection of the International Control Commission representatives. But as matters turned out, the representatives could receive complaints and other information only from natives within a very small area.

And those who complained always feared reprisals, which did occur frequently. The CIC representatives might have a truck parked alongside the council table and, after listening to the complaints of the people, might vote to allow them to leave and might tell the Viet Minh heads of the village of their decision. But that was not enough. The only way for a villager to be sure of getting out was to climb on the truck and leave immediately after the decision was reached. There and then. And the CIC could not furnish that much transportation.

Within the CIC committees there arose the same problems that arise in all conference bodies containing representatives of the Communists. The Poles seemed determined to be stumbling-blocks and I personally witnessed their obstructive tactics many times.

I would take a refugee to the CIC, a refugee who had been horribly beaten up by the Viet Minh. There would be a council meeting. The refugee would tell his story. After hours of wrangling, he would be sent back to the camp. It seemed that the Polish representatives always wanted proof that obviously was unobtainable. Certainly this poor peasant had been beaten—that could not be denied—but what hard-and-fast proof did he have that the beating had been administered by the Viet Minh? What proof did he have that the bullets which had torn into his arm were Communist bullets? The peasant would have to present some-

142

thing substantial in the way of proof, which of course he couldn't do, and not just his maimed body and feeble voice.

The movements of the CIC's mobile teams in Viet Minh areas were usually secret. That was so that nothing could be done in any particular village by way of a "fix." But a fix often occurred, nevertheless.

In October one of the mobile teams visited the city of Thai Binh, one of the largest in the Tonkin. The fix was in. There was absolutely no one in the community who had any objections to Communist rule. Every one of those who came to the council hearings had word of praise for the Viet Minh. Life was pleasant and the peasants were happy and the skies were blue. No one wished to leave. "Freedom" in the north was vastly superior to that life of bondage and subjugation in the imperialistic south . . . at least, such were the stories that went around the world about Thai Binh. It just happened that a great many photographers were present on that occasion, which also tied in with the visit of Prime Minister Nehru of India. There was also world-wide coverage by Communist and "neutral" newspapers.

Officers of the French Navy decided that perhaps they could do something in the way of a fix themselves. The French Navy did a great deal to help the refugees and deserves high marks for it. In this case, Captain Gerald Cauvin, the chief of the Deuxieme Bureau (Intelligence) drew up a plan.

Cauvin and I rounded up all the people who, we thought, might be of help, and the French Navy did the rest. The town chosen for our fix was Phat Diem, some fifty miles from Haiphong, behind the Bamboo Curtain.

Many of the refugees in my camp had told me that there were thousands upon thousands in and around Phat Diem who wanted to escape to the south, but could not. We chose the bravest and strongest among those in the camp who actually *had* escaped from that area, both men and women. We had them meet with Cauvin, some other French officers and me. It did not take long to gain their confidence. They were told of the plan, accepted their part in it and left Haiphong to cross back behind the Bamboo Curtain. Going behind the Curtain was not nearly as difficult as getting out in front of it.

Via this underground force, word was sent to the people of Phat Diem and the cantons nearby. "If you want to escape, gather in the church of the village of Phat Diem on November 1, the Feast of All Saints. If you go there, representatives of the CIC will visit you. You will be able to make your declarations to them, and perhaps gain your liberty."

The church at Phat Diem had not yet been closed by the Viet Minh. Ostensibly the people were to gather for the Holy Day of Obligation. And so they did.

From all the cantons in the area, thousands came to Phat Diem. People overflowed from the church into the mission yards. (All the missions in Indo-China have large court-yards in front and playyards around them for the inevitable nearby church school.) Here the people came to pray on the first of November.

Simultaneously, in Haiphong, and in other cities of Viet Nam, an intensive campaign got under way to persuade the CIC to go to Phat Diem and investigate the complaints that had "filtered in to us." Admiral Querville, General O'Daniel in Saigon, Admiral Sabin from his flagship at sea, Mayor Bot of Haiphong and many others sent notes and telegrams to the head of this particular mobile team.

But something went amiss. For reasons that I do not know—they were never explained to me—the members of the mobile team were unable to go to Phat Diem immediately. They could not go on the first, or the second or the third of the month.

Word was smuggled to the people of Phat Diem to wait, have patience, stay in the church, wait. Admiral Querville offered his own helicopter to the CIC men, though they had two planes of their own. There were more messages urging them to go to Phat Diem. And there was more delay.

The Viet Minh became suspicious. Why was this one Holy Day of Obligation lengthening into three? The Communists ordered the people to return to their homes. The people would not. The Viet Minh put guards around the church yard and forbade all and sundry to sell or give food or water to those within the mission walls. Let them have no food, no drink, just prayers; that is what the Viet Minh ordered. This starving-out process is a weapon of war dating back to the legions of Carthage, and doubtless to far earlier times. It was applied ruthlessly in Viet Nam in 1954.

Nevertheless, the people stayed. Only a few of the

weaker ones left. All the others waited for the representatives of the CIC, for they had faith in the word that had been sent to them. This patient race is not robust. Many are frail and susceptible to a variety of diseases. Yet their faith in their dream of freedom was strong enough to provide the nourishment they needed in this time of stress.

The days stretched out. Four became five, then six, then seven, and the hungry children cried. Mothers who were nursing infants dried up and were no longer able to feed. Hunger and thirst became passions. From lack of sanitation, disease got under way. Many became ill. Yet they waited—and prayed.

Finally, around the tenth of November, the CIC representatives went to Phat Diem. Members of the group told me later that they were nearly overcome with nausea when they got within a hundred yards of the mission. The odor of sickness was that intense. The Canadian members of the group said even the Polish Communists were amazed at the filth and squalor in which the people were huddled.

The CIC people took thousands of declarations, immediately ordered that the natives be allowed to eat and drink and move freely in and out of the mission. They sent vehement protests to the Viet Minh authorities and issued a public statement in Hanoi against the government of Ho Chi Minh and against his treatment of the people in the mission of Phat Diem.

In deference to world opinion, the Viet Minh ordered local authorities to allow the people to leave. But there was a trap even in this.

146

The Viets set up offices capable of processing one hundred people a day. One office issued passports, but only after sheaves of papers had been filled out by the applicants. Another office sold tickets for the Viet Minh busses, which reputedly would take the people to Haiphong. The tickets cost 8,000 Ho Chi Minh piasters each, the equivalent of about nine American dollars. For a peasant with a family of six, this represented a formidable sum of money.

But to people from different parts of the world who asked about this particular evacuation, the Viet Minh responded: "Yes, we are furnishing the bureaus, passports and transportation for all who—mistakenly, we believe— have decided to go to another zone. No sense of injustice, no hysteria, racks the Democratic Republic of the Viet Minh."

It was not until the 15th of November that the first group of refugees started to leave Phat Diem. Instead of bringing them up the road on a trip that would have required only a few hours, the Viet Minh sent them through a complicated itinerary. They took part of the trip on buses. Then they were stopped and told that the buses must be repaired and that they would have to spend several days waiting. During this period the Viet Minh lectured to them incessantly about the error they were making and about the American and French atrocity camps in Haiphong and Saigon.

Now the refugees were transferred to junks and sampans and floated up the Red River to Hanoi. More delays, more

147

haranguing, more frustration followed. From Hanoi, trains finally took them to Haiphong, where French trucks transported them the few remaining kilometers to our camp.

Thousands of other refugees went through all the delays the Communists could think of, finally to reach a point, far behind the Bamboo Curtain where it was noticed that their 15-day exit permits had expired. So they were sent back to the villages they had come from originally, there to attempt to start the evacuation process all over again.

Luckier refugees were picked up by the French Navy in small craft it had waiting at the very edge of the Bamboo Curtain, at the Bac Cuu. There the French stopped all Communist junks, and with representatives of CIC aboard, demanded that the people be handed over, so that they could be promptly transported to Haiphong.

In spite of the inconvenience and hardships, the maddening lectures, the inadequacies of transportation and the brutality of the Viet Minh, the people persisted. In Phat Diem alone, as was indicated by a final count before the CIC men left the area, about 5,000 of the original 35,000 gained their freedom.

CHAPTER XIII

BUI CHU MEANS VALIANT

Wars give birth to songs of warriors, to Rolands and to Arthurs. Wars give birth to legends of courage and valor, to Bataans and Inchons. Yet the strange new peace that came to the Tonkin brought forth innumerable instances of valor as great as any ever shown in combat.

I know a good many such stories. I have been an eye-witness to dozens and I have been told of hundreds more.

I remember the refugees from the province of Bui Chu who came to my camp in November.

Bui Chu is a province eighty miles from Haiphong. In Bui Chu, as elsewhere, under the "light" of Communism there was only darkness, and the family warmth died in the people's thatched homes. But the spirit of the people did not die, nor their hope.

The Tonkinese of Bui Chu were relatively rich. They had crops and water buffalo and little fields in the familiar green of the delta. Then came eight years of war—first a colonial war, then a war of ideologies. The wars brought desolation. Homes were destroyed, families broken up, crops taken. Water buffalo died and lands were made sterile. For the peasant the calamity was complete. His land, his ancestors and his family make up his whole life. He has nothing else, except his God.

Now new rulers gave the people new laws. They obliged these farmers to attend daily lectures on the evils and errors of capitalism and democracy. They preached hatred against the institutions, traditions and customs of colonial Viet Nam. Everything "feudal" or "reactionary" was to be destroyed. The concept of the all-important family was feudal and reverence for ancestors was reactionary. The whole province came to seem to the people like an immense prison. Their Christian catechisms were burned and they were told that religion is only an opiate. It was a life without comfort, without worship, without even enough food.

The promised agrarian reforms were carried out here as elsewhere. This meant that all who had more than two *mauu* of land (about as much as an athletic field) were considered capitalists and accused of exploiting the laborers who worked with them in the fields. When I asked such laborers if they were not pleased with gaining land, they would often say: "Sometimes it pleased our bellies but it never pleased our hearts because we knew it was wrong."

And, as has been said, because of increased taxes more land did not always mean more food.

The plight of the land owner who had many *mauu* of land was drastic. If he had a great deal of land, that meant he was comparatively wealthy and powerful, and if a man

150

is wealthy and powerful he cannot exist in the Communist state, unless, of course, he is a member of the party. Such people were sometimes given the choice of becoming members of the Party. If they did not consent, if they did not agree to give up their land and their religion and send their sons to serve in the "People's Army," they were apt to be beheaded. Do I exaggerate? The sons of such men have told me that they had witnessed the beheading of their own parents. I do not believe they lied.

For the people of Bui Chu there was only one answer, escape. Which was easy to hope for and dream about but very difficult to achieve.

There were more than 30,000 Catholics in Bui Chu province alone. In the Vietnamese underground, and in the French and U. S. Navies, a plan was laid. Date and hour and place were decided upon. The date was November 30, and the place was a spot off the shores of the province near the fishing village of Van Ly, a village known for its long, broad beaches.

A large French repair ship, the *Jules Verne,* stood off the shore just outside the three-mile limit. Then four LSMs pulled alongside the *Jules Verne* for imaginary repairs. By planned coincidence one of the United States Navy's large transports, the *General Brewster*, was passing empty from Saigon on her return trip to Haiphong. At this spot, she too stopped for a little while.

The Vietnamese underground had spread the word to the people. At the escape hour minus ten, the sea was uneasy. On the three-mile stretch of churning water from the ships

151

to the shore there was nothing to be seen but the moonlight, and that was too bright . . . too dangerous. Then the escape hour arrived, eight o'clock. Within minutes the sea was a veritable mass of bumboats, barks, and bamboo rafts.

Thousands of escapees appeared on the beach and dragged their boats across the sands into the tide. They headed out to the small French craft which were speedily spreading in toward them.

French and Vietnamese met and the French craft opened their bow doors wide and silently engulfed the refugees, many times raft and all. Then the French craft turned around and raced out to the *Verne* and the *Brewster*. They disgorged their loads of pitiful people and returned to pick up more.

On a small bamboo raft lashed together with rope and perhaps only a few feet square, there might be as many as ten members of a family in their brown cotton garb, drab, quiet, frightened. If the weight of the load made the raft submerge, sometimes until the sea was around their knees, they would hold their children up high.

The moon was bright. Would it give them away? The sea was rough. Would it capsize their boats? The big ships were but two. Would they be enough? Did the enemy yet suspect? Would machine gun fire soon cut loose and give frenzy and terror to the night.

These fears gnawed at the Vietnamese as they aimed their crude boats toward the open sea. But they were truly valiant and all risks were taken, including the risk of death. By dawn there were 6,000 escapees on the U. S. and French

152

ships, which then set out for Haiphong. There they discharged their loads into our camps and returned to Bui Chu for more.

Operations continued for two days and nights until the number of escapees numbered more than 18,000. On the third day no refugees appeared on the beaches, save for a small group stranded on a sand spit. Soldiers appeared and the escape from Van Ly halted.

But not the dreams of those who remained imprisoned there. Another time would come; there would be another chance. They would try again.

When the ships came to Haiphong bearing these particular refugees, they were unloaded at the piers by night and day. We would transport them to the entrance road of the refugee camp. It is a half-mile walk from there to the tents. The first night when the refugees arrived the trucks let them off just at the entrance. Lining each side of the entrance road, shoulder to shoulder, stood thousands of refugees who had arrived on earlier nights and days. Most of them held lanterns or candles. The newly arrived would walk between these lines of flickering lights in a poignant parade of pathos.

They were scanned by other refugees seeking word of relatives, perhaps of sons or daughters, and they were bombarded with weary and usually hopeless questions.

"Have you seen any of the Duc Ly family?"

"Did you see anyone swim away from the capsized Quan boat?"

153

"Have you heard what happened to the village of Thanh Hoa?"

"Have you seen my son? He is seven."

Some did find relatives and friends. Most did not.

In days and weeks following, while people from Bui Chu lived in the camp, they required constant medical care. Many of the children were hideously scarred from bouts of smallpox. Others had the new pustules of the epidemic form. Perhaps secondary infection had set in. Their fevers raged. Dehydration racked their small bodies, and I lost three or four a day to this one disease alone.

Beri-beri and scurvy were common. In part, at least, these vitamin deficiency diseases owed their existence to the Communists' so-called land reforms. They brought starvation to many, though not enough to kill, just enough to maim.

Beri-beri would make their ankles puff and swell until their feet became so tender it was impossible for them to walk. The skin would pull tightly over the swollen ankles and would tear with the slightest shock. Many could not wear their sandals or walk on even the softest ground.

Scurvy made their bones brittle and fractures were seen at every sick-call. Gums became rotten and teeth decayed and broke off.

My corpsmen often walked through the tents at night giving injections of morphine to those in the most excruciating pain. But when thousands of such cases came upon us suddenly, we had to ration relief from pain; there were just not enough morphine-like drugs in all Haiphong for us to do otherwise. Penicillin is the drug of choice for yaws, and fortunately America had sent me plenty of this. We treated more than 200 cases every day, 200 bodies disfigured with stinking sores on the hands and feet and face.

Starvation left many scars, for example on the babies with their swollen bellies. All who had escaped had become seasick and this enfeebled them the more. These miserable people who had fled to our camp were now my patients.

The people of Bui Chu, I found, are not unlike my fellow Americans. Americans never fail to like the Vietnamese when they get to know them. It is impossible not to respect their driving compulsion for freedom, impossible not to admire the story of such a valiant people as those of Bui Chu. The main difference between them and us is that we have our freedom and our hearts command us to keep it. The Vietnamese does not possess it and his heart's command is to struggle against all odds to achieve it.

And so the escapees continued to flood into our camps like the monsoon rains, spilled and overflowed into the adjoining roads and fields. As soon as possible we processed them to the transports. Every day we embarked four to five thousand, but they often came into the camps faster than that.

This was my camp's population. My city of sprawling tents staked out in knee-deep mire and mud. We were thriving—with vermin, filth, disease, and death. Yet ours was a camp of hope and pride, and a camp rich in tales of heroism.

155

CHAPTER XIV

THE ORPHANAGE OF
MADAME NGAI

Although daily life at the camp was far from dull, there was a certain monotony, born of repetition, in our existence in Viet Nam. Day after day, week after week, month after month, we saw the same diseases, the same misery. We experienced the same shortages of materials, the same lack of help.

Worst of all, we had the same sense of inadequacy, the feeling of being unable even to scratch the surface of the despondency all around us. Combine this with the personal discomforts, the lack of hot water and clean clothes, the withering heat, the continuous sweating, the necessity of speaking always in a foreign language—and you get some idea of the continuous effort that each day's task demanded.

There was no place to go and say, "The devil with it," no place to put your feet on a table, drink some gin and tonic and read the funny papers. Our constant companion was misery. If we did knock off for an afternoon, a sense of guilt would fill us and the afternoon's pleasure would be gone.

Sometimes, when there was a U. S. Navy Ship down in the river, we would go out, bum some hot water for a shave and pass an hour or two with our own people. The men on those ships will never know what it meant to my boys and to me when they let us use their quarters as our temporary home.

Towards the final months of the evacuation, these occasional visits to U. S. ships became real highlights. The *Cook*, the *Diachenko*, the *Bass*, the *Begor*, the *Balduck*— these small APDs looked as grand and glorious as the *Queen Mary* to those of us who worked ashore. Their sailors and officers with their friendship helped me keep some level of sanity.

However, there was another highlight in our Haiphong life. This was the orphanage of Madame Vu Thi Ngai, the orphanage of An Lac.

This orphanage and its hundreds of smiling children became *our* orphanage and *our* children. We really sort of adopted them, as they adopted us. Madame Ngai was the head of the place and my corpsmen and I became the Orphanage Medical Department. The U. S. Navy became the Orphanage Trust Fund. If this sounds a bit involved, I can only say that it became more so as the months went by. Whenever there was an opportunity, the kids would be taken out to one of the ships, where they would be given an American-type party.

Madame Ngai was a proud Tonkinese woman who had

once been wealthy. She was lovely, with fine-textured skin, jet black hair, brilliant white teeth and an olive coloring that was exquisite. Her eyes were broad and wide, with that charming Oriental slant that quickly captivates so many.

She was large. Like many women who run orphanages, she had and needed room for a capacious heart. Nature had designed her bosom bountifully so that she might the better accomplish her essential task—that of loving children. Madame Ngai succeeded in capturing the hearts— and the wallets—of all she met, and she succeeded in meeting not a few. Especially Americans with large hearts or large wallets, or preferably both.

There was only one other person in all of Viet Nam who was charming as Madame Ngai, and that was one of her wards, little Lia. Let me tell you about Lia. Lia was a seven-year-old girl who was as delicate and as pretty as only the perfect doll-sized Oriental can become. She had fine little features and a complexion that seemed almost transparent. She was shy, but not too shy. And when she grew fond of you, how very fond she grew!

Lia was one of the older girls of the orphanage and busied herself caring for the infants as well as she could. But there was one thing wrong with Lia. She had one leg, and where the other had been she had a short stump. Her right leg had been blown off at the thigh when she stepped on a land mine in January of 1954 near the town of Phuly. The explosion made her an orphan as well as a cripple.

For a right leg, she used a rough-hewn wooden crutch. I met Lia when I first went to the orphanage in August.

After some time, she let me examine her stump. It had healed poorly and there were raw granulating surfaces on it even six months after the traumatic amputation. I asked Lia if she didn't want to let me take care of the stump for her. She replied that she did, because she loved the *"Bac Sy My."* So we started a little campaign. With some minor surgical procedures, secondary closure of the wound was obtained. Then Lia did all the things I asked. She stretched the stump, exercised it, soaked it, kept the dressings on and kept it clean. As a result, she had a good functional stump by Christmas.

I wrote to Henry Sherck of the A. S. Aloe Company of St. Louis, told them Lia's story and asked for help. Their response was refreshing. Although they could not themselves supply the artificial limb that I had asked for, they did consult with the Hanger Limb Company, which is in St. Louis also. The two outfits decided that the man to manufacture this new leg was at the Cosmevo Ambulator Company of Paterson, New Jersey. They told me the measurements they wanted and we sent the information along. And so a limb was made that would be suitable for this little girl, a limb that could be adjusted to her growing. Some time later, the limb arrived in Haiphong.

Lia now had a new leg, an American leg. Her eyes glowed when she put it on and walked for the first time. She cried and smiled and then cried again (and so did Baker, and Madame Ngai, and so, I confess, did I). Gratitude spilled out of Lia's eyes until she couldn't say thanks —and didn't have to.

Alas, Lia's leg brought moral problems to the orphanage. The little girls of Viet Nam ordinarily wear long black pants down to their ankles but, to show off her new leg, Lia most of the time went around pantless. Though the children were mostly very young, this still proved to be embarrassing, and we had a devil of a time trying to get Lia's pants on. She was so enamoured with her leg that she even slept with it. When we asked her not to, she was puzzled. She did not take off her Vietnamese leg when she slept, she said, so why should she take off her American leg?

Mr. Cosmo Invidiato, head of the Cosmevo Company, recently wrote to tell me that, in effect, his company had recently "adopted" Lia. "To judge from your letter," he wrote, "and from what can be read between the lines, conditions must be horrible for the inhabitants of that faraway country. Somehow it is difficult for us back home to understand the sacrifices and hardships that other people are continuously undergoing. Sometimes we fall to musing on our uselessness." I can tell him his firm wasn't useless to little Lia.

Another child we all loved very much was Nguyen. We never knew his last name. Madame Ngai said she found him, when he was four, in the village of Thai Binh. Nguyen was now six, had a winning smile and a caressing face. Nguyen had tuberculosis of the spine and was a misshapen hunchback. It was difficult for him to walk, so he waddled. He could not sit down comfortably and would lie down to eat his meals. When he laughed very hard, which he did

160

wonderfully and frequently, he would fall to the ground on his back and roll. Nothing seemed to stop him from keeping up with the others; when it came to visiting an American vessel, he was by all odds the best man about the ship. I believe he has a collection of some fifteen sailor hats which were given to him or, more often, swiped by him.

There was a two-year-old child whose name I do not remember. He had had trachoma infections in both eyes as an infant and now, at the advanced age of two, was totally blind. If he had had a minimum of medical care during infancy, he would now be able to see. But this he was denied, and so he will live in darkness forever.

There were other children who had the bony deformities of congenital syphilis, others who were cerebral palsy cases, or spastics, or otherwise diseased. Some were really pitiful to behold, even for a case-hardened doctor. They had seen death in hideous forms, and had felt its shock and horror. They had witnessed villages pillaged, fields destroyed, and had known the stink of decaying dead. But, to the young, God gives the blessed clouds of forgetfulness and soon the bestiality of their background faded. So the children of the orphanage smiled, and they loved, and they made life seem good and complete.

The way Madame Ngai would thank those of us who were fortunate enough to have the chance to help her was to invite us over for dinner, which for some of us greenhorns sometimes was a secretly frightening experience. It was always a true Vietnamese dinner. Please have some

161

more bat-wing soup, rice, of course, in all its forms, fish heads, chicken served with the head on, sparrow eyes crushed and made into a paste, raw pork with sauces, that damn oil made from decaying fish, salad—where from, Oh Lord, and how well washed?—and other foods which were, surprisingly enough, pretty tasty even to American palates. (I ask you not to consider their origin and development.)

During dinner we would squat on our haunches or sit on pillows on the decks. Buddhist joss sticks always smoldered in colored jars of sand. There were usually a few Vietnamese and French officers present. But politics and war were barred from the conversation. The differences between colony and mother country, between America and France, between white man and yellow man, between JGs and, let's say, Lieutenant Commanders—all were excluded from or dissolved at Madame Ngai's fluid parties. At one of the parties we asked her to tell us how the orphanage was born. Where did she find all these children? Where did she get the money to feed them? Who were they?

Like many of the people of her race, when recounting a story Madame would speak as though retelling an ancient legend. She spoke as if in a dream:

"In 1946, in the village of Thanh Hoa in southern Tonkin, there were many great battles. Families were split. Dead littered the village. Children were abandoned on the roadways to die alongside the bodies of their parents. Wars do not have time to stop to take care of the infants.

"I lived in Thanh Hoa. In fact, at one time my family

162

was the wealthiest of all in the canton. I had a lovely large house with many *mau* of fields around it. Although much of my home was destroyed in battle, I was still able to live there. I went along the roadways and took the children who, I found, were still alive, and brought them from the ditches to my house. My servants and I took care of them.

"But when another battle started in Thanh Hoa, we knew we would have to escape. So, with my brood, I left. I took my jewelry and the gold cubes that I had and went to the nearby village of Nam Dinh. Here I bought a new house and continued to care for the children, whose numbers had now swollen to six hundred.

"When Nam Dinh fell to the Viet Minh in 1949, I was forced to move again, only this time with a thousand children. Those moves I repeated five times, finally settling here in Haiphong.

"The Mayor of the city gave me a fine building to house my children and the city helped to support them. But at the beginning of this year, the year of Dien Bien Phu, the French needed my building for a hospital, so I was obliged to move to the house we occupy now. I should be ashamed to entertain you in such a common house, and yet it is my home, and so I am not ashamed. This is how I came to be the mother of a thousand children.

"My own husband was killed in the first month of the war, and my two children are living in France. I have never really left Tonkin, and many say that I am so French I am almost colonial. I do not hate the French. I know they

163

have done many good things for my country. The language
that we are speaking now is French.

"But my people are confused. They do not know the
value of things, of friends, of foes. And that is how I
came to be."

After she told us her story, we understood more than we
had understood before. Yet there was so much, so difficult
to understand, in this land. The buildings she had were
inferior and, by our standards, inadequate. The main house
was a small, perfectly square building, with two rooms on
the first floor and two on the second. Although it did have
electricity (one bulb in each room), it had no plumbing or
any other modern fixtures. Behind the house there were
two other buildings which were sleeping quarters for the
children. There were four rooms on each floor and about
twenty children slept in every room. Then there were
several large open areas with tin roofs over them and
with many hard wooden beds. Here the other hundreds
slept, and during the monsoon rains, canvas was dropped
over the sides to prevent wind and water from entering.

The funds Madame used to run her orphanage were her
own or were acquired mysteriously. The clothes she gave
to the children were sometimes those she was able to charm
from some French Admiral or General—for example,
Admiral Querville.

Admiral Querville, the Commanding Officer of the
French Navy, at one time in 1954 had a surplus of navy
blue uniforms. At a large French dinner party, with a
surplus of good wine, Madame Ngai, with a surplus of

bosom, beguiled Admiral Querville out of some of his surplus uniforms. They were then cut up and down and made into small suits for her children.

When General René Cogny, Commanding Officer of the French ground forces, captured a Viet Minh warehouse full of Communist uniforms, Madame Ngai heard of it. At the next dinner party, General Cogny was put to the same test undergone by Admiral Querville, and again Madame Ngai's orphanage come out the winner.

The orphanage was prospering. Madame Ngai loved every child, and smothered them all with great tenderness and devotion. Her children were good and well-behaved Buddhists.

The Americans entered her life in August of '54 when the small landing force arrived in Haiphong to set up the funnel's mouth for the evacuation of the refugees. The Military Assistance and Advisory Group (MAAG) had several officers there under Colonel Hamelin, USA, and Colonel Victor Crowziat, USMC. Mike Adler was there as head of the United States Overseas Mission. My boss, Dr. Amberson, and I were on hand too. It did not take long for Madame Ngai to find us—or perhaps for us to find Madame Ngai; I don't remember which it was—and we were soon completely conquered by her goodness and by the smiles of her herd of kids.

Madame Ngai had never met another American save one —a flier downed during the Japanese occupation, whom she had hidden in her home. Although she spoke exquisite French, the only words she knew in English were "Yes, thank you very much." When we told her that this expression lacked variety and might even be dangerous at times, she would smile and say in French, "There is no need to say anything else."

When Captain Amberson left Haiphong, his last words to me were: "Don't neglect those kids at Madame Ngai's." That was one of Captain Amberson's orders that Dooley tried to obey to the letter.

Dr. Amberson had started sick-call at the orphanage and I was able to continue it until April 1955, when the outfit moved to the south. Sometimes, after dinner, while the Frenchmen regaled their hostess with tall tales, I would take my bag and make the rounds in the big house of the orphanage and in the outlying sheds. Many of the children were undernourished, though desperately well cared for and well scrubbed. In fact, there was enough disease and infirmity among these kids to give a man a complete residency in pediatrics, and they made my professional visits busy ones. But there was always time for a romp or two, particularly with my pal Nguyan.

I bummed a lot of things off the ships for the kids, and the ships gave a lot spontaneously. But I couldn't keep using Navy funds earmarked by Congress for whitehats in order to help orphans in Viet Nam. Medicines had to be acquired in some other way.

I wrote again to the Mead-Johnson Company of Evansville, Indiana. I told its executives of the orphanage and reminded them how, during my years in medical school, they had sent me samples of their various vitamin products at least once a month. I asked them if they would now send me enough vitamin "samples" to provide adequate daily doses for six hundred children for six months. They responded by sending me enough vitamins for about a thousand children for a year.

The children took this medicine as they were asked to, though I do not believe that the fish taste and the sour aftertaste in their mouths contributed much to their love of America. But, whatever the taste, their health improved a great deal.

At the University of Notre Dame, at South Bend, Indiana, there is a lady whom many students have come to know and love. I was one. She is my second favorite lady at the University of Notre Dame—Notre Dame herself is first. I wrote Erma Konya, telling of the orphanage of An Lac, this time begging for clothes. As a result of that letter, Erma began sending a package of clothes a month and is continuing the practice now that the orphanage is in Saigon. Each package contains fifteen or twenty small, colorful T-shirts, some small socks, shorts, some combs, perhaps some lollipops. One time there were a few pairs of bright colored suspenders. The kids wore these around the waist like belts; they didn't like them the other way.

Often when a U. S. ship would come up the river we would ask the captain if he were agreeable to a children's party. If the answer was "Yes," at two o'clock in the afternoon we would pile thirty or forty children into a truck, drive them to a pier and load them on a crash boat which would take them out to the ship.

167

By the time they arrived, the children were usually a little wet and always very noisy. They would have an hour of comic movies, then cookies and ice cream (this usually gave them diarrhea). A sailor would be assigned to each child and it was a toss-up as to which of the pair had the better time. After the movies and the banquet, the children would entertain the sailors. They would sing Vietnamese folk songs or do ancient Tonkin dances. The older boys would demonstrate judo. A single crew member would find ten uproarious children all attempting to throw him at once. Obligingly, he always ended up on the mat. The kids completely captured the hearts of the sailors, and when they left the ship their hands and pockets were full of candies and cookies, their stomachs were full of ice cream, their hearts and eyes full of love and wonder—and they usually wore the sailors' white caps.

Many of the sailors had bought colorful scarves in Japan to take home to their girls in America. Mysteriously, these began to appear on the heads of the Vietnamese orphans of Madame Ngai.

One LST which gave the kids a party was used as a heliport for the Commodore's helicopter. The Commodore intended to take the helicopter out to the Baie d'Along on official business. He had planned to hop off at 1330, but since the children would not arrive on ship until 1430, the Commodore was easily persuaded to wait until then. That would enable the children to see the helicopter take off—a most thrilling and memorable sight indeed to these Vietnamese orphans. The children enjoyed it tremendously,

168

and the dignified Commodore seemed to enjoy their enjoyment. At any rate, he waved so frantically he almost fell out of his helicopter.

Mornings, when we would load refugees at the embarkation zone, Madame Ngai would come and bring half a dozen of the older children. They would help the refugee children of Viet Nam to carry their bundles and sometimes carry the refugee children themselves. They would help the mothers with their baskets and their balance poles. Madame Ngai would pass out bread to the refugees, bread that had been bought with American Aid money and cut up to make small sandwiches. Madame Ngai, and Madame Querville, wife of the French Admiral, passed out more than 700,000 loaves of bread to embarking refugees while I was in Haiphong, which is a formidable number of loaves in any language.

Whenever something was needed at the orphanage that could not be found in the city, which was dying a little more every day, we would turn to the USN. We could always ask whatever Navy ship happened to be in the area for whatever was needed, from nails to napkins, food to floorboards.

Some ships contributed canned and powdered milk. Others contributed cuts of meat. Many took up collections. On the *Balduck*, with her crew of fewer than 120 men, more than $200 was collected and given to the orphanage as a Christmas present. The *Cook* collected over $200 also, in addition to contributing the usual sundries, including pencils and toothbrushes. The sailors would buy such articles in the PX and send them to the children as gifts.

Commodore St. Angelo, who was the Navy "boss" in the middle months of the Evacuation, took an interest in the orphanage and decided that the children should learn some American sport. Somehow or other he hit upon ping-pong, and he had the ship's carpenters build a table for the kids. One of the junior officers on his staff, Lieutenant Al Moses, wrote to his wife in the States and had her send paddles, balls, and a net. Soon the orphanage resounded with children howling and scurrying after the ping-pong ball. And it wasn't long at all before Madame Ngai could beat all comers.

When things were not going too well at the refugee camp, when the mandarin in charge wasn't getting things done as well as could be expected, I would go to Madame Ngai and tell her my troubles. She would jump into my jeep, ride out to the camp, and in no uncertain terms straighten things and people out.

I remember one time when we had just completed a big clean-up campaign, getting the refugees to clean and burn and in general to shine up the camp a little. Now the chief mandarin and some of the lesser officials were getting difficult, as we all did from time to time. Madame Ngai cornered some of them and began ranting: "This camp is filthy. Never saw it look so bad. Why aren't you helping the American doctor to keep your own camp clean?" I thought the camp looked cleaner than it had looked for months, but decided to hold my tongue.

Madame Ngai had the spirit and fight of a girl of sixteen, though she looked to be about thirty and was actually nearer sixty.

When was the orphanage going south? We kept raising the question, fearing that she and the children might be trapped. "Not yet, not yet!" was her answer, week after week. There were still children coming into her home who needed her. She would hold on until the last minute. This caused concern among the French and Americans, who never lost apprehension that Ho Chi Minh might "liberate" Haiphong before the official date in May of 1955.

By the middle of April, however, the city was plagued with Communist riots and demonstrations, and Madame Ngai at long last made up her mind that the time had come for her to move on. Arrangements had already been made in Saigon by the United States Overseas Mission. A building had been found and the American Wives Club of Saigon was waiting for this fabulous woman to appear. They had heard of her and her kids from every acquaintance of their husbands, who had ever visited Haiphong.

So, in the middle of April, the orphanage moved, in toto —beds, mats, planking, pierced steel plating used for floors, desks, bassinets, barrels of chopsticks and rice bowls, small sewing machines, coolie hats, blankets, rice, vitamin pills, artificial leg, ping-pong table and everything else. At that time it sheltered about eight hundred children.

Commodore St. Angelo had me send Baker south with the orphans to make sure they were well treated on all sides. He returned to me a week later; during his absence

171

it was a rough week for me. Admiral Querville personally supervised proceedings when they went aboard an LSM early in the morning, and, before the sun rose over the Red River, the children were on their way down to the bay to be transferred to the *General Brewster* for their Passage to Freedom. After the two-day, three-night voyage, they were met by the American Wives Club and taken to their new home in Saigon's shaky safety. Meanwhile, Madame Ngai's American "orphans" in Haiphong sighed with relief for her sake—and suddenly felt very lonely.

Madame Ngai had never before been out of her beloved Delta. The fact that she had to abandon it represented a personal loss as well as a national tragedy to her. She often spoke of her belief that the Tonkin would be regained.

"We Tonkinese are a militant people," she used to say, "much like those Texans you have told us about. We know that we will some day wrench our land back from the Viet Minh. Of this there is no doubt."

With women like this in a nation, faith and hope in it will persist, whatever the temporary chaos.

.

172

CHAPTER XV

COMMUNIST RE-EDUCATION

The children of Viet Nam become old very young. They are mature and grave while still in early adolescence, and they are often very brave.

A number of them worked for us in the camps, staying on for months. They did adult work, accepted adult responsibilities; when they could bum cigarettes, they even smoked like adults. Yet they were only eight, or ten or twelve years old.

Each of my corpsmen had six or seven such young assistants. The badge of honor was a white sailor hat. A retinue of them followed me around day and night, sometimes to my embarrassment. They might come to me and lead me to a feeble old woman who could not leave her tent, or take me to see a man who was crippled. They would run errands for me, fetch things I wanted, boil water for the sick-call tent. Sometimes they did my laundry, but on such occasions they were apt to wash the clothes in a rice paddy, and the *wrong* paddy at that, so I discouraged this. And sometimes they would ride my truck just for the fun of it, as children should.

During the months when I was living in Haiphong hotels, they would sleep outside my door. They were often the go-betweens when newly arrived escapees needed help immediately.

Whenever Mr. Ham or any other Vietnamese official wanted to see me, he would spot one of these kids with the sailor hats, or one of the shoeshine boys, and tell him to "find the Bac Sy My."

When one of my assistants would leave for the south we would hold a little ceremony. Various ships' officers had given me their Ensigns' bars. So, on the official day, the Quan Hi, or Lieutenant, would commission his assistant a Quan Mot or Ensign in the U. S. Navy. A bar was pinned on him and his sense of self-importance increased so you could notice it. I hope the Personnel Department of the Navy will be understanding when it hears about my unusual recruiting service.

The Viet Minh directed much of their propaganda at the children and adolescents of the nation, and they went to unbelievable lengths to drive the propaganda home. The first time I ever saw the results of a Communist "re-education" class was during the month of December. What had been done to these children one December afternoon was the most heinous thing I had ever heard of.

Having set up their controls in the village of Haiduong, Communists visited the village schoolhouse and took seven children out of class and into the courtyard. All were ordered to sit on the ground, and their hands and arms were tied behind their backs. Then they brought out one of the young teachers, with hands also tied. Now the new class began.

In a voice loud enough for the other children still in the classroom to hear, the Viet Minh accused these children of treason. A "patriot" had informed the police that this teacher was holding classes secretly, at night, and that the subject of these classes was *religion*. They had even been reading the catechism.

The Viet Minh accused the seven of "conspiring" because they had listened to the teachings of this instructor. As a punishment they were to be deprived of their hearing. Never again would they be able to listen to the teachings of evil men.

Now two Viet Minh guards went to each child and one of them firmly grasped the head between his hands. The other then rammed a wooden chopped chopstick into each ear. He jammed it in with all his force. The stick split the ear canal wide and tore the ear drum. The shrieking of the children was heard all over the village.

Both ears were stabbed in this fashion. The children screamed and wrestled and suffered horribly. Since their hands were tied behind them, they could not pull the wood out of their ears. They shook their heads and squirmed about, trying to make the sticks fall out. Finally they were able to dislodge them by scraping their heads against the ground.

As for the teacher, he must be prevented from teaching

175

again. Having been forced to witness the atrocity performed on his pupils, he endured a more horrible one himself. One soldier held his head while another grasped the victim's tongue with a crude pair of pliers and pulled it far out. A third guard cut off the tip of the teacher's tongue with his bayonet. Blood spurted into the man's mouth and gushed from his nostrils onto the ground. He could not scream; blood ran into his throat. When the soldiers let him loose he fell to the ground vomiting blood; the scent of blood was all over the courtyard.

Yet neither the teacher nor any of the pupils died.

When news of this atrocity came across the Bamboo Curtain, arrangements were made for escape, and soon teacher and pupils were in Tent 130 at Camp de la Pagode.

We treated the victims as well as we could, though this was not very well. I was able to pull the superior and inferior surfaces of the tongue together and close over the raw portions. The victim had lost a great deal of blood and, as we had no transfusion setup, all I could do was to give him fluids by mouth. He could not eat anything solid, not even rice. For the children, prevention of infection was the important thing. Penicillin took care of this, but nothing could give them back their hearing.

The purpose of this book is not to sicken anyone or to dwell upon the horror of Oriental tortures, which we recall from World War II and from Korea. But I do want to show what has come upon these people of the Delta. And justice demands that some of the atrocities we learned of in Haiphong be put on record.

176

One midnight, shortly before Christmas, I was awakened by knocking on my hotel door. Two young boys asked if Bac Sy My would please go with them right away. I thought they were from the camp, and that there was something there that needed my attention. So I quickly dressed and went out to the truck. As we were heading out the road, the children motioned for me to turn off onto a path running between two rice paddies. I didn't understand, but they were so earnest that I followed their directions. We turned and drove several hundred yards to a straw paillote, or round hut-like building.

I bent, entered the low door, and then noticed first how dark it was and secondly how unexpectedly large it was inside. There was a kerosene lamp burning in one part of the hut and near it were several kneeling figures—an old man, an old woman, several boys—chanting prayers in a quiet monotone.

They greeted me with "Chao ong, Bac Sy My," clasping their hands before them and bowing their heads, in the Oriental fashion. Then I saw that there was a man lying on a straw mattress which in turn was atop eight or nine long pieces of bamboo, making a crude stretcher. His face was twisted in agony and his lips moved silently as though he were praying, as indeed he was.

When I pulled back the dirty blanket that was over him, I found that his body was a mass of blackened flesh from the shoulders to the knees. The belly was hard and distended and the scrotum swollen to the size of a football. The thighs were monstrously distorted. It was one of the

177

most grisly sights I had ever seen. The idea of merely touching this man was repugnant.

I felt queasy, knew I was going to be sick and rushed outside. Inside that hut I had just seen a masterpiece of systematic torture. Under the sky, I retched and vomited my insides out. I was grateful that no one followed me; they understood and were patient.

I am not sure how long it took for me to get hold of myself, but I finally regained enough nerve and stability to go back and care for this human nightmare. But what could I do? For his pain I could give him morphine. For the belly I could do little, as the skin was not broken in more than four or five spots. All the bleeding was sub-cutaneous, in bruises which were turning a purple-yellow. I put a large needle into the scrotum in an attempt to drain out some of the fluid. Later I would insert a catheter into the bladder so that the patient could urinate. What else could I do?

I asked the old woman what on God's earth had happened to this poor human being. She told me.

He was her brother, a priest, from the parish of Vinh Bao, just on the other side of the Bamboo Curtain. Vinh Bao was not more than ten kilometers away from Haiphong.

The area had been in Viet Minh hands for only about seven months and the Viets had not yet completely changed the pattern of village life. The priest was permitted to continue celebrating Mass, but only between six and seven o'clock in the morning. This was the time when most of the peasants were just ready to start the morning's work

178

and, under Communist rule, this was the hour when people had to gather in the village square for a daily lecture on the glories of the "new life."

This meant that they were unable to attend the parish priest's Mass either daily or on Sunday. So, for the few who dared to risk his services, the valiant 57-year-old priest held them in the evening. The Communists decided that he needed re-education.

Late the night before, Communist soldiers had called at the priest's chapel, accused him of holding secret meetings and ordered him to stop. Defiantly he replied that nothing could stop him from preaching the word of God. And so this is what they did: they hung him by his feet from one of the crude wooden beams under the ceiling. His head was so close to the ground that he later said, "Frequently I would place my hands on the ground to try to take the pressure off my feet."

With short, stout bamboo rods they proceeded to beat the "evil" out of him. They went on for hours; he did not know just how long. They concentrated on the most sensitive parts of the anatomy. "The pain was great," the priest said. It must have been very great indeed.

He was left hanging in the church and early the next morning his altar boys found him there and managed to cut him down. They were only eight to ten years old, and they ran to their parents, attending compulsory classes in the square, and sobbed out the news.

The parents told them what to do and then said good-bye to them, knowing that it might be good-bye forever. The

179

children lashed together an arrangement of bamboo poles that could be carried as a litter and floated as a raft. They put the priest on this and carried him down the back lanes of the village. They hid him near the bank of the river, which formed one of the boundaries of the free zone. After dark, they lowered the raft gently to the water and, with three on each side, paddled to the middle of the river where they were swept into the down-river current. The coolness of the water probably did more for the priest than most of my medicines. They managed to get him across the river to the free zone without being seen. Arriving late at night, they carried the man to the hut of his sister. Then they came to find me.

I made daily visits to him thereafter and gave him antibiotics and more morphine. Miraculously, he survived; his own strong constitution and no doubt his faith brought about a cure.

Sooner than I would have considered likely he was sufficiently recovered to be taken to Camp de la Pagode. Although he was still crippled, he was soon saying daily Mass and teaching the children their Catechism; in fact, for a time he served as the camp's more or less regular chaplain.

Perhaps I should have let him do it when he insisted that he must return to the village. Perhaps the world needs martyrs, although Tonkin, I thought, had an oversupply already. Next time the Communists would have killed him for sure.

I know that it is not just to judge a whole system from

the conduct of a few. However, this was Communism to me. This was the ghoulish thing which had conquered most of the Orient and with it nearly half of all mankind. From December until the last day, there were two or three atrocities a week that came within my orbit. My night calls took me to one horror after another.

Early in my Haiphong stay I was puzzled not only by the growing number but by the character of Communist atrocities. So many seemed to have religious significance. More and more, I was learning that these punishments were linked to man's belief in God.

Priests were by far the most common objects of Communist terror. It seemed that the priests never learned their "Hoc-Tap Dan-Chu," their "Democratic Studies and Exercises," as well as they were expected to. This meant that they had to be "re-educated" more severely than others. It is difficult to take men whose life had been dedicated to belief in God and straighten them out so that they no longer believe in God. In fact, most of them proved unconquerable.

Catholics have many pious ejaculations which they utter frequently—"Jesus, Mary and Joseph," for example, and "Lord have mercy on us." The Communists ordered the priests to substitute new slogans for them, for example, "Tang gai san u xuat" (Increased Production), and "Chien tranh nhan" (The People's War). Perhaps the expression most often heard in the conquered north was "Com Thu" (Hatred).

The Communists have perfected the techniques of torture, inflicting in one moment pain on the body and in the

181

next pain on the mind. When Tonkin spring came and the monsoon ended, I thought perhaps nature might bring a change in the tenor of things. I was wrong. On the first Sunday of March, I was asked by Father Lopez of the Philippine Catholic Mission to come visit a "sick man," a priest who had just escaped from the Viet Minh.

We walked across the huge sprawling courtyard to the living quarters. In a back room there was an old man lying on straw on the floor. His head was matted with pus and there were eight large pus-filled swellings around his temples and forehead.

Even before I asked what had happened, I knew the answer. This particular priest had also been punished for teaching "treason." His sentence was a Communist version of the Crown of Thorns, once forced on the Saviour of Whom he preached.

Eight nails had been driven into his head, three across the forehead, two in the back of the skull and three across the dome. The nails were large enough to embed themselves in the skull bone. When the unbelievable act was completed, the priest was left alone. He walked from his church to a neighboring hut, where a family jerked the nails from his head. Then he was brought to Haiphong for medical help. By the time of his arrival, two days later, secondary infection had set in.

I washed the scalp, dislodged the clots, and opened the pockets to let the pus escape. I gave the priest massive doses of penicillin and tetanus oxide and went back to the mission every day. The old man pulled through. One day when I went to treat him, he had disappeared. Father Lopez told me that he had gone back to that world of silence behind the Bamboo Curtain. This meant that he had gone back to his torturers. I wonder what they have done to him by now.

Priests were not the only victims of brutality. One day an old woman came to sick-call in the camp. She was wearing a cloth bound tightly around her shoulders in a figure-of-eight. We removed the cloth and found that both the collar bones had been fractured. En route to the camp, she told us, she had been stopped by a Viet Minh guard who, for the crime of attempting to "leave her land," had struck her across the shoulders with the butt of his rifle, ordering her to go back home. This fractured the bones, making her shoulders slump forward and causing excruciating pain. Nevertheless, she managed to escape. In time, with medical care and a regimen of vitamins, she healed.

Always there was the painful thought: "My God! For every one of these who come here, there must be hundreds or even thousands who could not escape."

One day a young man came to sick-call with a marked discoloration of the thumbs. They were black from the first joint to the tips. He was suffering from gangrene, of the dry type, called mummification. There was no great pain, no blood, just raw necrosis of tissue.

He said he had been hung by his thumbs to "re-educate" him. This had happened about a week earlier, and since then his thumbs had been getting a little darker every day. Now they were beginning to smell.

183

During the course of the examination, while I was manipulating the left thumb, a piece of it actually broke off. There was no bleeding, no pain; there was just a chunk of his thumb that stayed in my hand. This dried piece of flesh, like that of a mummy, had crumbled away with the slightest pressure. The circulation had been cut off for so long—he said he had been left hanging for days—that permanent damage had been done, and all the cells and tissue had died distal to the point where his thumbs had been tied with cord.

"But remember, my friend," one of the elders said to me, "these people might never have left the north if the Communists had not done these cruel deeds against those who preached and practiced their religion."

I feel sure he was right. There were many Buddhists among the refugees, but when I thought of the attendance at daily Mass I had no doubt that 75 or 80 per cent of them were Catholics. Of the 2,000,000 Catholics in Viet Nam, about 1,750,000 lived in the north. Then came the Communists and inevitable disillusionment with the promised reforms. Perhaps they could have borne up under the oppressive taxes, the crop quotas, the forced labor and the loss of freedom. But when the right to worship God was taken from them—often by the most brutal means—they knew it was time to go.

"What fools they are, these Viet Minh," the elder said. "They coax the people to stay, tell them lies, and even try to stop them at the perimeter. Then they do the very things

184

that will drive the people into exile! Perhaps it is the will of God!"

To say that the Communists tried to stop the refugees at the perimeter was to put it mildly. Though under the Geneva agreement anyone had a right to leave the north who wanted to, the Communists began to violate the agreement on this point from the day it was signed.

As I have indicated earlier, they employed trickery, threats, violence and even murder to stop the southward rush of their subjects. "It is my duty," said Premier Diem in Saigon on January 22, 1955, "to denounce before the free world and before Christendom the inhuman acts of repression and coercion taken by the Viet Minh against the populations wanting to leave the Communist zone, acts which are flagrant violations of the Geneva agreement."

The Premier later estimated that a quarter of a million more would have left if there had been no harassments. My own belief is that this figure is not half large enough. The unbroken flow of the luckier, and of the wounded and mangled who made it to the American camps, was a clue to how many failed to make it. Besides, it is reasonable to assume that thousands who thirsted for freedom lacked the courage or the vitality to take the risks.

Many and various were the Communist devices to keep the people in the north. They made it illegal for more than one member of a family to travel on a bus or train in the affected area at the same time; or for more than two persons to go on foot together on the roads pointing to the evacuation zone. This made it difficult for would-be refugees, whose families were large and held by powerful bonds of unity, to break away.

Nevertheless, desperate parents often sent their children ahead, two today, two tomorrow, with instructions to get to the American camp. By the dozens and the hundreds I saw youngsters, alone, exhausted and sorrowful, arrive and settle down on the fringes of my camp to wait for their elders. Many a time they waited in vain.

In many parts of the Tonkin the Communists ruled that special passports would be required—not to leave the country; that would have flouted Geneva too crudely— but to cross from one canton into another. Obtaining the passports involved steep fees and fantastic red tape. But only with such documents were the refugees permitted to travel as family groups.

Having at long last received its passport, a family might set out on foot on the long road to Haiphong. Fifteen or sixteen days later, their food almost gone, sore and perhaps sick, they would reach a canton line. They would run into that old dodge of the expired passport.

The Communist guard would examine their hard-won document and laugh. "Comrades, this passport is good for only fourteen days. Didn't you know that? Oh, you can't read? Well, anyhow, go back and get a new one."

As a leftover of the war, many roads were sown with mines and booby traps. The victorious Communists dug them up. But often they did not detonate them. Instead they tossed them with designed casualness into rice paddies, swamps, and bushes close to the perimeter of our evacua-

186

tion area. If citizens trying to crawl to freedom at night were blown to bits, it only served them right.

Yet here are the terms of the agreement: "Any civilians residing in a district controlled by one party who wish to go and live in the zone assigned to the other party shall be permitted *and helped to do so* by the authorities in that district." Those italics, of course, are mine.

CHAPTER XVI

LEADING THE LIFE OF DOOLEY

Reveille for Dr. Dooley and his small band in Haiphong was 5 A.M. I shaved in a basin of cold water, brushed my teeth with chlorinated water brought from the camp and dressed, all in a matter of minutes. My standard working clothes—and every day was a working day—consisted of khaki trousers or shorts, a T-shirt and a uniform shirt with the sleeves cut off.

Never did I neglect to wear my collar insignia and my Navy hat. These, especially the hat, were important. Symbols mean a lot in the Orient. To the hundreds of thousands who passed through my hands, the bars on the collar and the eagle on the hat stood for authority, true, but also for friendship and for that whole far-off nation called the United States. My corpsmen and I were determined to impress upon the people that what we were doing for them was being done through the generosity and love of the American people.

"Yes, the gloves on your hands are good," a refugee might say. "But the eagle on your cap is bad."

"No, the eagle on my cap is good," I would answer. "Without the eagle there would be no doctor-gloves. The eagle stands for America. America sends the Navy, which brings you the American Navy doctor. And the American Navy itself takes you to safety in Saigon."

These arguments went on interminably at sick-call. Sometimes I wished it were possible just to work without talking. But this job had to be done.

Almost always I found one or two boys sleeping in the corridor outside my door and a few more sprawled in my jeep. There would be a few of these "little Dooleys" at my heels when I appeared, at a little after five, either at the camp or in the village church, for Mass.

After Mass, breakfast. Usually I returned to my quarters, where I made instant coffee on a hot-plate and drank it, with crackers. (In the earlier months, in the few remaining shabby restaurants, French and Indian, I sometimes treated myself to more substantial fare.)

By six o'clock or a little later, I was in the Medical Tent for the day's first assortment of tropical ailments, fractured limbs and suppurating wounds. Patients queued up before my arrival, and there was still a line by the time I knocked off for lunch.

For that, I might head for the orphanage, where Madame Ngai was sure to fix me a hot meal. Wherever I went, I usually brought my own water, since I couldn't afford to be too sick too often.

By one o'clock I tried to be back in camp for the serious business of learning Vietnamese.

At three, when the temperature dropped to a more tolerable 100 or so degrees, I resumed sick-call. However long

189

the lines, I had to crowd in visits to the hospital tents for checking, treatments and sometimes surgery. This carried me to 5:30 or 6 P.M., at which time I drove my jeep to other areas where our people were quartered, including a warehouse in town which housed thousands of them.

Dinner, too, might be contributed by the orphanage. Then, by eight or thereabouts, I was back in my room for a cold sponging and bed. There was a prayer in my heart that I might be allowed to sleep through until morning. But often my young guardian angels would be obliged to waken me. Someone's condition had taken a bad turn, or new atrocity victims had arrived for patching.

Such was the basic pattern. This, of course with many variations, was the life that I led from the end of August till the middle of May. It melted off fully a third of the 180 pounds I had arrived with. The routine went on despite several bouts of malaria, four different types of intestinal worms, and a mild but uncomfortable case of acne. My hands were dyed red, because I did not have much alcohol to use as a cleansing solution but did have plenty of tincture of merthiolate. After I left Viet Nam, it took a week to bring my hands to near normal.

The drain on my energies never really bothered me profoundly. I was young, had a sound constitution and was a sound sleeper. The psychological strains were harder to manage. Try as I would not to let the sorrow and savagery bother me, the goad of conscience drove me to do more and more, and the stabs of guilt reminded me that I could not do enough.

190

Toward the end of my assignment, I seldom went out to the ships in the bay. It was a four hour trip by small boat. With the Viet Minh itching for trouble, our launches made no trips after dark and the daylight hours were my busiest. But the lure of a hot shower and a decent meal often seemed irresistible. Once I succumbed to the lure, and sent a message, via my walkie-talkie, requesting the command ship's helicopter.

When the skipper asked me what was up, I answered boldly: "Sir, I am in desperate need of a hot bath and a decent meal." He merely chuckled.

Actually the whole task force knew about Dooley's bathing difficulties, having heard about the time I went aboard the flagship and was invited to luncheon in Admiral Sabin's cabin.

I was wearing a battered khaki shirt and trousers, my hands were stained red with merthiolate, and I needed a bath. Nevertheless, with all those high-ranking officers present, the Admiral seated me at the foot of the long table, directly facing him. I was obviously flattered, but he brought me up short.

"Don't get any ideas, Doctor," said the Admiral. "You just smell so bad I want you as far away as possible."

I would soon see a time when my heart was so heavy that I grasped like a child at anything that was good for a laugh. I even began to look kindly on Baker's clownish pet baboon, despite the fact that he was chewing the seat covers off our truck.

191

CHAPTER XVII

THE DYING CITY

The months passed but the refugees continued to pour in week after week from all the provinces of north Indo-China. Some days we would get fewer than a hundred; other days there would be thousands. They came by boat, by land, by foot, by junks and sampans.

Camp de la Pagode was taken down in March and other camps were erected. During January and February, we had three huge camps with a total capacity of over 30,000.

Eventually all of my Navy corpsmen left except Norman Baker, the dauntless interpreter who did everything else but interpret.

It was at that luncheon given by Admiral Sabin that I made a clean breast of the Baker affair. "You see, sir," I said, "I speak French, and now I speak Vietnamese, so I hardly need an interpreter. But Baker is a wonderful all-around assistant. So I've been holding on to him under false pretenses."

"Well, well," the Admiral said, assuming a mock-serious

expression. "I hate to disappoint you, but you weren't fooling us. I knew all along you were pulling a fast one."

It turned out there were a lot of other fast ones that he hadn't minded either. There had been complaints about my habit of lifting supplies from ships in the area. "Look what Dooley's done now—60 drums of oil and he just signed his name for it! Who the devil does that boy think he is?"

"Well," the Admiral would say, "I'm sure he wouldn't have taken the stuff if he hadn't needed it urgently."

Also, he had become inured to my rare but high-handed raids on ship personnel. For example, at a time when I was acutely short-handed, I requested that four volunteer corpsmen be given TAD (Temporary Additional Duty) with me. Since their Captain had no desire to release them, I sent a message directly to the Admiral. It must have reached him, for the four men were soon at work in my camps.

Many months after our talk on his flagship, I received a letter from Admiral Sabin commending me on having been awarded the Legion of Merit. In it he wrote: "The Book says the Lord will help those who help themselves and it seems to me that, in the evacuation of Indo-China, you, Dr. Dooley, several times managed to give the Lord a nudge."

Not once did the Admiral fail to endorse my nudging. I had superb support from on high, and without it I would have been licked.

By April the push began to slow up. Evidently the new

193

masters of north Viet Nam had plugged most of the remaining holes in their Curtain. The French Army was almost gone, along with its equipment, quonset huts, tanks, office furniture. Only a few hundred French soldiers were still encamped on the nail of the finger-like projection of Haiphong. Operation Cockroach, my end of the more elegantly named Passage to Freedom, was entering its final stage. Once, when a helicopter was sent from a ship for me, the Communist perimeter was already so choking-close that the plane had to land on a small lot in town.

Haiphong was dying. Every day more shops and houses were deserted. Only a few civilian vehicles remained of the thick motor traffic we had found on arrival. The reeking bazaar which had fascinated me was burned "by accident." There was little doubt that it was the work of Viet Minh infiltrators.

The few officers of MAAG left, except an Air Force Major, Ralph Walker. Roger Ackley, replacing Mike Walker toward the end, brought some new ideas and the camp administration was revamped.

Major John McGowan, U. S. Army, was the Military Attaché who stayed on until the very last day. He was another excellent type of career officer who did his job with all his heart, withstood all discomforts and managed to retain his sense of humor. I was lucky to have men to work with like John McGowan. They were a constant inspiration —and a constant gig in the rear. When I felt myself slipping, becoming lazy, I would see other Americans in Haiphong doing their jobs well, and then guilt would get me. "Up and at 'em."

By now my evenings were spent either at the camps, talking to the refugees, by this time in their own language, or in town, at the abandoned bank building (the coolest place in town) where John and I would argue big subjects like Army versus Navy and bigger ones like wine and women. We would consider it a treat when relatives would get mail through to us and we would have a copy of *Time* or *Newsweek*. The Embassy in Saigon sent a plane up with our mail once or twice a month. This was always a great day.

We had used an amazing tonnage of DDT, plus thousands of gallons of Lindane, and other insecticide solutions. The water systems had worked overtime and now I believed they should be put out to pasture in the green fields of North Carolina.

All the city people who intended to leave were leaving or had left. By this time, most of those remaining in the city could be assumed to be pro-Viet Minh, if not actually full-fledged Communists. It was now that real trouble began.

The Governor's staff and the Mayor's staff left, with only skeleton crews remaining. All was grim and silent on the streets. Violence became common in the "new society" about to install itself on the ruins of Haiphong. The first riots exploded in the second week of April.

It seems that several hundred Viet Minh trucks arrived with so-called refugees piled high in back. These refugees did not want to live in the camps; they wanted to move into the city, where there were hundreds of empty buildings.

As the trucks tried to drive across the Ha Ly Bridge leading to the city, the French stopped them and forbade them to enter, saying that the Viet Minh were not to take over completely until May 19, and that this was beating the Geneva deadline. The truck occupants argued that as refugees they could enter at any time.

Tempers became short on both sides. The bogus refugees pushed across the bridge and the French soldiers poured out tear-gas bombs. Hand-to-hand fights developed. Several of the "refugees" were killed, hundreds were wounded, including many soldiers; and the Red radio broadcasters in Hanoi had themselves another propaganda holiday. Such clashes became ever more frequent.

I had one more difficult task to perform. The shoeshine kids were still in the city, and still my friends and protectors. One time my camera was stolen when I foolishly left it in my truck, parked on a side street. I told the artful dodgers of my loss. They were furious to think that anyone would steal from their American doctor. I think they were also furious to think that other people were horning in on their own purloining territory. Within a few hours my camera was returned. They said they had found it. I wondered whether one of the lovable, larcenous kids had probably stolen it himself without knowing to whom it belonged.

The time had come for the shoeshine kids to go. I consoled them with assurances that the shoeshine business was certain to be lush in Saigon and that a good thief, like a religious man, finds it hard to survive in a police state.

What convinced them finally, I think, was the matter of shoes. The idea came to me in a flash one day. "Well," I said, "you might as well throws those kits away. There will be no more shoe-shining when the Viet Minh arrive. Or do you think you can shine canvas shoes?"

They looked at me suspiciously, and then at one another. I wasn't kidding! From their frequent forays behind the Bamboo Curtain, they had learned that canvas sneakers were standard equipment among the Viet Minh.

At that point they agreed to be vaccinated and dusted with DDT. One April morning, Baker and I boosted a few of them into a truck and went downtown to gather up the rest from the street corners. We gave them each a loaf of bread and a final delousing and watched them shoulder their shoe-shine kits and file sullenly aboard the landing-craft. They arrived safely in Saigon, and I'm sure that city hasn't been the same since.

On May 10 the Viet Minh staged another proof that the American doctor and Americans in general were hated by the population. Our green truck was stolen. It was a one-ton truck Doctor Amberson had gotten from the Haiphong Public Health people. They had received it from the French, who got it from the U.S.A. through American Aid. I used it for ten months, for every conceivable mission. It had been turned on its side in a riot and, in another demonstration, had had all its windows broken. The spare tire, the cap of the gasoline tank, the windshield and the light bulbs were missing towards the end. Baker's baboon had eaten most of the interior, yet the spunky little truck still ran. The monsoon rains had done their best to make it moldy. You couldn't sit down in it with clean trousers and come out looking the same. Yet the little chariot could go anywhere, haul anything, and was well known throughout the city. To make sure that no one forgot it, Mike Adler had the big American Aid insignia painted on its side.

On the tenth of May it was stolen from a parking space near the bank building. Late that night we found its charred and blackened chassis in the town square. The Viet Minh apparently had burned it in a public demonstration to illustrate to the Americans that they were despised and to the Vietnamese that the new Democratic Republic of Viet Minh would have nothing to do with anything "made in the U.S.A."

I was as depressed as if a friend had been murdered, and for a moment thought of having what was left of the chassis buried with military honors. USOM officials in Saigon probably are still filling out chits to account for ONE TRUCK, DODGE, ONE-TON, GREEN.

The Catholic Mission was now about empty. The nuns, the school children and all the priests except one very old native had been sent south. Sun-burned Father Lopez had packed up his bicycle and departed on the *General Brewster*, taking his one clean cassock and his intestinal worms with him. Father Felice, who always looked so jaundiced in spite of my vitamin pills, antibiotics and phenobarbitol, left on an embassy plane in the last week of April.

I hated to see them go; they had become good friends. They were made with hearts of that proverbial precious metal and they had been wonderful to our small tribe of Americans. It was Father Felice who offered early Mass every morning in the Mission Church, usually full of bare-foot chanting natives. He tells me he could usually determine when I arrived because of the way my boots squeaked as I made my way to the very front row.

The old native priest who was left in charge would say Mass until Haiphong fell, and intended to try to continue even after the Viet Minh took over. He knew that he might be made to suffer but he said that he was old and that a martyr's crown might ensure his entry into Heaven. Haiphong's last weeks found his Masses attended by a dwindling handful of the devout.

The pride of the Mission was their statue of Our Lady of Fatima. Several decades before, when Haiphong Catholics were in Rome on a pilgrimage, His Holiness the Pope had given it to them with his blessing. It stood on an altar of its own just to the left of the main altar. It was an object of popular reverence, with flowers and burning candles always around it. Day and night peasants prayed before it.

There were many discussions about the advisability of removing the statue of Our Lady of Fatima. Should it be taken south when Father Lopez and Father Felice left Haiphong? Should it be kept until the very last possible

199

day? Or should it be left to give comfort to the few who might, for one reason or another, remain behind?

In the end, the decision about the statue was made by an American, Norman Poulin. Roger Ackley was called back to Germany toward the very end and our embassy flew Norman up to succeed him. Norman spoke impeccable French. His job was to help wind up the final details of the evacuation. He was charged especially with getting out the American equipment that remained north, the tents, the few vehicles, some American Aid rice, and other products which USOM was determined not to leave behind for the use of the Viet Minh.

The last American embassy plane flew in on the eleventh of May, the main airport had gone to the enemy, so it landed on an abandoned military airstrip. The pilot of the plane had a message from Father Felice. He asked: "Is the statue of Fatima all right or have the Viet Minh defiled it?"

Norman met the plane and received this message. I was there hoping there would be a message for me to get on this plane and get the hell out of Indo-China. (There wasn't.) We held a short conference and made a quick decision. We sped to the Mission in the jeep, which was on its last legs. We buttonholed the poor old priest and tried to bamboozle him. "We want the statue. We want to send it south on the embassy plane."

The old priest shook his head. "Oh no, it must stay."

We failed to convince him and at last we pretended to agree. "Very well, perhaps it must stay."

200

Then, as he tottered back to his cubicle, we went into the church on the double. We climbed up on the little altar and literally kidnapped the statue. We wrapped it in an American Aid blanket which was on the jeep's floor and whisked it out to the airport. At this writing it is standing in a church built especially for the refugees, just outside Saigon. And that's how Our Blessed Lady of Fatima, with a boost from American Aid, made the Passage to Freedom.

When people ask when the heart of Haiphong stopped beating, the date I give them is the fourth of May. It was on the fourth of May that, according to the treaty, an advance echelon, the Viet Minh Committee of Experts, was allowed to enter the city. They were to go to the City Hall, the Governor's office, the public utilities plants and so on and learn how to take them over from the Vietnamese, the last of whom would leave on the sixteenth of May on the last boat out. Thus there would be no sudden cessation of water or electricity and, in theory at least, the turnover of the city would be smooth.

The Committee arrived, 480 strong, in brand-new, Russian-made Molotova trucks. They were impeccably dressed in high-collared grey uniforms, pith helmets and canvas shoes, and most of them spoke French very well.

They stopped me about four times daily, when I was trying to cross a street, or drive out to the camp or go down to the docks, but they were always polite and respectful. They said I was the only American they had ever met who could speak their language. Why had I learned it? Did I intend to stay on and try to help the "true people of Viet

Nam" when the Democratic Republic established its offices? I replied that my job was just about over and that I expected to be leaving soon.

They sent a delegation out to the camp and gave me a bit of dialectical materialism.

"When you treat people in America," the leader asked, "do you make any distinction between Democrats and Republicans?"

"Certainly not!"

"Very well," he said. "There must be no distinction here between capitalistic dupes and the loyal people of Viet Nam."

Then the cheeky bastard ordered his men to divide up my pharmaceuticals and surgical supplies—half for me and half for the Democratic Republic of Viet Nam. And there wasn't a thing I could do about it.

I tried to be polite with the newcomers but perhaps I merely gave them the impression that I was afraid of them. And I was. I was constantly afraid that they would lock me up somewhere and hold me for investigation. Investigations can stretch out for years in Communist states, as many an American knows to his cost. And we were only four Americans in all of north Viet Nam.

The arrival of the Committee of Experts was not bad in itself. But trouble arose because, when they arrived, they brought several thousand armed bodyguards with them.

The bodyguards raised hell in the village. When they arrived, riots, fires, "spontaneous" anti-foreign demonstrations, and beatings of men and women who had been friendly to us became common. The newcomers cynically blamed all these things on the French.

There was a riot in front of the City Jail and the Committee of Experts demanded that all prisoners be released immediately. The French replied that they would be released on the sixteenth of May, according to the agreement, and not until then. This demonstration ended up in tear gas and firing on the crowd.

I climbed up in the steeple of the Mission one afternoon and looked all around the city. You could see little puffs and clouds of smoke in seven or eight parts of town, where demonstrations were being broken up with tear gas. The French used it frequently as the last violent method of dispersing mobs.

The forces of General Cogny, keeping cool heads, did a good job at keeping some semblance of order during these last weeks. As for me, I spent most of my time dodging riots, driving blocks out of my way to get to my objectives, so that I would not be stopped and questioned. A good deal of the time I spent just being afraid.

By the 10th of May we had taken down the tents of our camps and moved the remaining refugees into empty buildings in the city. It was on the twelfth of May that I saw my last grisly atrocity.

By this time the Viet Minh legally had all but a very small area on one side of Haiphong, but illegally they had just about all of it. Their strength was visible everywhere. They patrolled the main streets and waterways, and there were sentries at every intersection. They captured a young

Vietnamese boy, a wild type of lad, who still wanted to escape from Viet Minh territory and dared to try.

He attempted to duck through back streets across the line of demarcation, known as the DMZ or Demilitarized Zone. Here he was apprehended by the Viets. They formed a circle around him and beat on his feet with the butts of their rifles. They continued this until the victim collapsed, then added more blows for good measure, all on the feet and ankles. This was what was to happen to runaways in the future!

The Viets stopped beating the boy only after he was unconscious. When he regained his senses, he found that he had been left alone and that the road was abandoned. He dragged his shattered, mangled feet into a nearby alley. There a rickshaw driver found him and somehow got him across to us on the free side.

I had no X-ray equipment but it was obvious that the damage was beyond repair. The feet and ankles felt like moist bags of marbles and were already gangrenous. I had only a few instruments left and a little procaine and penicillin. I did the best I could by disarticulating the ankles where they connect with the lower leg. Someone else would have to do a more thorough amputation job later. We managed to get the boy into a crash boat which took him out to a French LSM, waiting to sail for the south. He was crippled for life, but at least he was free.

Our last loading day was the twelfth of May, a dry hot morning. The shuffling of thousands of bare feet made acrid dust rise off the ground at the loading area. One could taste the dust. It made the tongue feel thick and the teeth gritty. There was little sound except for the chugging of the LST motors. We were still spraying the refugees with DDT.

A May morning in America means spring, softness, sweet odors, perhaps a cool misty rain. But here the heat of the Indo-China sun was intense, the glare of the river was blinding and the smell of the refugees was overpowering.

This was the last day of the last loading. Some 3,600 refugees would take the trip, first to the bay and then on to Saigon, huddled together with their cloth bags, their balance poles with household possessions at each end, their babies on mothers' hips. They were as desolate a slice of the human race as any that had preceded them. They walked slowly in line to be dusted with DDT, to accept a loaf of bread, or perhaps a few diapers and small bags of clothing. But to me they were not a mere mass of wretchedness. I had come to know their valiant hearts and stout spirit. Somehow, over the bitter months, without knowing how it happened, I had identified myself with their dream of life in freedom and their tragic destiny. They had become my suffering brothers.

Of course these last refugees were not really the last. There were still a couple of million behind the Bamboo Curtain who never had a chance. But we had done the best we could. And I hope the men who made the deal at that lovely Geneva lakeside are happy with the results.

I had been taught to believe in and do believe in God's love, His goodness, His mercy. And I knew that in some small degree at least these qualities can be shared by man. But I had seen very little of them in the last year.

"I must remember the things I have seen," I said to myself. "I must keep them fresh in memory, see them again in my mind's eye, live through them again and again in my thoughts. And most of all I must make good use of them in tomorrow's life."

I watched the last LCT pull away from the dock and, as I came to the full realization that it was all over, a quiet grief engulfed me. The boat headed downriver and an enormous sun was sinking in a burst of splendor.

CHAPTER XVIII

AFTERWORD

Why did the refugees feel about us, America, as they did in the years before Dien Bien Phu?

It should be remembered that every rumbling tank that overran the villages of the Tonkin, every blazing napalm bomb that seared the huts of the natives, every gun and jeep and truck and uniform that brought havoc upon the people in what they considered a "colonial" war—all these were "made in the U.S.A." The people of North Viet Nam considered the United States as a vast warehouse and supply depot for France's colonialism, as indeed we were. I don't know the exact figure, but it was in the hundreds of millions of dollars of aid, in military materials, to France for the war in Indo-China.

This equipment from us was laden with propaganda potential on both sides of the Bamboo Curtain. But only the Viet Minh Communists took the initiative. Perhaps it was because many Americans consider the word "propaganda" a dirty word. ("Information" is more acceptable.)

Perhaps it was because, by its very nature, the cogs of a democracy turn slowly. In any event, the Communists didn't lose a moment.

The Viet Minh had a well-staffed and extremely effective psychological warfare department, under the leadership of General Giap, the man whose army conquered Dien Bien Phu. The propaganda was directed not at the leaders, not at the mandarins, not at the government heads, but it was directed at the common laborer of the delta. And the propaganda succeeded horribly well.

In the areas that had been under the Viet Minh control for five, six and seven years, the propaganda did little good. These people knew by the emptiness of their bellies that the Viet Minh was a fraud. The illness of the minds of their Communist re-educated children proved to them that the new system was evil—much more evil than France had ever been. But to those in the areas that had only been recently conquered, or turned over to the Viet Minh through the Geneva Treaty, Communism still held a fascination.

They were attracted by many of its ideas, especially the promise of land reforms. The people of Viet Nam had borne the burdens of colonialism for over eighty years and they were weary of them. The Communists offered the allurements of a "new way of life." The Democracies offered nothing, though they had the greatest things to offer—justice and freedom. I do not mean to imply that Communism was "voted" into power, but it did not meet with intelligent, or indeed any other kind of opposition.

The people from the two zones never met face to face.

One of the first rules of the conquering Communists was to restrict travel. As a consequence it was difficult to spread the truth about the "new way of life." And to those disillusioned people from the old zones who got through to unconquered ones the response would often be, "Well, when the Viet Minh liberate *our* areas it will be different. We shall work harder to produce the paradise that they have promised. The reason your province is in anguish is because you are too slow, you cannot work long hours, you take siestas, you do not toil the fields long enough. Things will be different when *our* province is rid of the French yoke. . . ."

One might ask why, if they were so much in favor of the new rule, and if they so hated Americans as an extension of their French colonial rulers, did so many of them attempt to escape to Haiphong? The answer is simple. For the greatest majority of the refugees, utilizing American ships was just the lesser of two very imminent evils. The first evil was the suppression of their religion. The second was that of risking one's life on an imperialist American ship.

The Viet Minh suppressed their religion. The Viet Minh closed their churches. The Viet Minh put priests and ministers to the fields to work, or killed them. All outward manifestations of religion were destroyed. Because of this, and not because of anything we did, they decided that it would even be worth the risk of contact with the Americans, in order to gain what they knew was religious freedom in the South under Ngo Dinh Diem.

As I have tried to show, when the Tonkinese arrived at our camps their emotions ranged from deep hate to mild distrust. Very few refugees arrived wholeheartedly joyful that they had reached the threshold to their passage. Instead they arrived fearful, apprehensive, and sometimes absolutely antagonistic. At first they accepted everything, from penicillin to their daily bowl of rice, with marked reluctance.

At the start the refugees associated only terror with a uniform. However, they were soon learning to associate help and love with our work. I wanted to be sure they realized that our love and help were available just because we were in the uniforms of the U.S. Navy. The reason we were there to help them was because we were in the service. That is why Baker saluted me, and called me Quan Hi, which means Lieutenant, rather than Doctor. Everything we did was done because the American Navy made it possible for us to do it. Soon we began to feel a quiet pride in our hearts at being Americans. We had come with ships to take them to freedom, with medical aid to heal their ills and bind up their wounds, with large supplies of life-saving drugs freely donated by American firms merely on my say-so. We had come late to Viet Nam, but we had come. And we brought not bombs and guns, but help and love.

The two groups that inspired me to write this book were at diametrically opposite poles of civilization. That stinking mass of humanity under foreign skies, those miserable and diseased people who in the depths of anguish had hearts

210

so splendid and a faith so powerful, were my first inspiration. The other group were my friends in the Navy—the fifteen thousand sailors and officers who gave such touching and tender care to the wretched of Viet Nam. They did this without orders, simply because they wanted to help people who "didn't have it so good."

A finer lot of men cannot be found anywhere on this earth. When they encountered the problem, they asked for an explanation. When it was explained, they understood. When they understood the suffering, they decided to alleviate it. And they *did* alleviate it. They conquered the hearts of every one of the refugees who sailed on our ships. They did this with an enthusiasm and wholesomeness that defies description.

Certain ships stand out in my memory as superb. First the *Montague*, AKA 98; then the little APDs, the *Balduck*, 132; the *Cook*, 130; and the *Diachenko*, 123. Lastly the gawky LSTs, 885 and 1096. Certain men, Pete Kessey HM3, Norman Baker ABM3, Dennis Shepard HM3, Commander Le Forge, and Lt. Johnny Fusco, Lt. Johnny Walker and Lt. H. S. Hayden, and the inseparable Lts. Ted Torok and Hal Zimmerman, the excellent Commodores, especially Captain Walter Winn—these I remember.

My understanding and very patient boss, Admiral Lorenzo S. Sabin, USN, who must have spent many hours wondering just what the devil his Lieutenant (junior grade) was doing in Haiphong that was a little legal. I was always borrowing equipment, demanding supplies, and acting as though I had four more stripes than I wore. I was usually illegitimate and out of channels. But the Admiral backed me all the way. His staff men—Lt. Floyd Allen, Major N. R. Smith, and cigar-chewing Major John Kelly—helped me with everything from logistics to chow.

Lt. Pat Ledwidge, Ensign Charlie Rush and Lt. Bob Athout put up with me, lent me clean clothes, and gave me plenty of boosts when my morale was sagging. Lt. Don Stibich, in spite of his youthful face and soul, was a truly fine man, and a constant inspiration to me to become as good as he seemed to think I already was. Lt. Al Moses, one of the most genuine men I have known, gave me stability when I needed it; I needed it frequently.

Commander Wendell Mackey quietly infused some patience into my Irish breeding which I needed when my mob required a touch of "diplomacy." Lt. Tom Avertt I remembered especially because he loved the children of Madame Ngai, and did so much in their behalf. Some civilians too gave me intangibles, Mike Adler and Roger Ackley especially. Air Force Major Ralph Walker, a confrere of Haiphong, gave me more than he received from me.

One other name shines forth—Army Major John Mc-Gowan. A military man through and through, a true Christian and a real philosopher, he spent many a night explaining principles and military ethics to me. He took vague concepts which I could not catalogue and helped me with them, gently probing me to think further, examine and analyze. He could define terms like Communism, war, dialectical materialism, death. He would knead and mould

212

my mind, and mature my reasoning. He would always lead me to a just decision. We seldom talked that he wasn't really teaching, without ever seeming to do so. To him I owe a great debt. If there is anything creditable in this book, to him goes much of the credit; thanks, John.

When I returned to the hospital in Japan at the end of the Indo-China experience, I weighed less than 120 pounds, and with a six-foot frame this looked rather lean. Commander Charles Mann of the Medical Service Corps took one glance at me, and offered me two weeks leave. He gave me something else—two orders: (1) eat plenty of raw steak, and (2) write a book. With tongue in cheek he *ordered* me to write. Charlie, here is the book I promised.

To the typists with their ceaseless work goes my gratitude, especially to Elmo Mims and to Joe Polifrone.

Passing through Hawaii on my way home, Captain W. Lederer, USN, well-known in the editorial and publishing worlds, gave me a real boost. He pushed the appropriate buttons, and found my publisher, and therefore gave me the platform from which to tell my Viet Nam story.

Silas Spengler and Joe Albanese, though never in Viet Nam, had an understanding of the situation down there, and an understanding of this doctor's work. And they knew my sadness. They spent long hours helping me to form this manuscript, advising me on it, and never losing confidence in me, even when I direly lacked it myself. Being with them I felt as though my head was in the sky, high and clear, but my feet firmly planted on God's earth, staunch and sure. And for them my heart has much gratitude.

And finally and perhaps the most important of all, Lt. Norton Stevens, USNR, deserves my deepest thanks. He who served with me in Indo-China, and again with me in Japan during that rocky period when all was over, and so much seemed confusion. Nort sat with me many a night and would say, "O.K. Tom, just slow down, take it in your stride, you'll be fine. Soon you will see the splendor of the thing again. Now there is only depression from what you have witnessed. In time you will see the glory of it." Thanks to you, Nort, now I do see what you spoke of those foggy nights in Japan.

The best that I can say of all those men is that they are good Americans. The best that I can say of myself is that I can call them my friends. If apologies are due for some of my erratic ways, then I ask them to remember that

> "The woods are lovely, dark and deep,
> But I have promises to keep,
> And miles to go before I sleep."

U.S. Naval Hospital
Bethesda, Md.

CPSIA information can be obtained at www.ICGtesting.com
Printed in the USA
BVOW04s0326201213

339480BV00011B/902/P